Stay In Your Lane

Dr. Toluleke Famuyiwa

Dedication

This book is dedicated to everyone who desires and works toward discovering their unique gifts and purpose with the intent of dedicating the rest of their lives to it. The journey is a process, and we can all use some guidance.

Acknowledgements

I am grateful to the many individuals who helped make this book a reality. I cherish my loving wife, Tasha Famuyiwa, for her support and encouragement throughout the writing process.

I greatly valued the support of my parents and siblings, especially Mrs. Omolola Sobiyi, who helped to proofread this book.

I called on the wisdom of my friends Aditya Devender, Adenmosun Olumide, Dr. Ayomikun Soyombo, and Luiz Bravim, for their guidance and feedback on this book.

I appreciate the support of my mentees, Davian Caraballo and Zoey Bowers, for revising this book.

I owe a special thank you to Kate McClare from Kate's Copy. Kate is a skillful and talented writer. She has years of experience in writing from different walks of life. She helped me to make this book wonderful by identifying omissions and making necessary textual additions.

If you are reading this book, I am thankful for the investment you have made in yourself. I am certain that this book will give you the small push you need to live life at your maximum capacity.

Table of Contents

Introduction

I sometimes wonder how a simple man like myself, from a very humble background, could end up leading a life of impact and influence. My childhood was not filled with a lot of privilege, my parents were okay financially, at least enough to provide basic education for my siblings and me. However, with the paucity of resources and opportunities in Nigeria, it is necessary to look at my journey critically and acknowledge that things have gone quite well.

As I write this book, I have a thriving career in academia and just completed my PhD in Integrated Biology from Florida Atlantic University – I have been awarded the McKnight Dissertation Fellowship from the Florida Education Fund, as well as the Graduate Fellowship for Academic Excellence from the Graduate College at Florida Atlantic University. I consider myself to be in the beginnings of life as my research and teaching interests flourish. I continually surround myself with a thriving network of influencers, friends, and family who all love me. I also cherish my marriage to my loving and supporting wife.

My journey is ongoing, but there's a lot to be grateful for. It is for this reason and many others, that I consider it important and urgent to share the nuggets of wisdom I have acquired over the years and throughout my personal pursuit for success. Thus, I designed the book, *Stay in Your Lane,* to help people create patterns for success and achieve more than I have achieved.

The phrase *"Stay in your lane"* connotes living according to your values, gifts, passions, and ultimately your person. Like the Shakespearean quote declares, "to thine own self be true." Unfortunately, many people are not clear as to what their talents are, much less know where to invest them. This is unlike people such as Hollywood actress Marsai Martin, tech entrepreneur Steve Jobs, Former President of the United States Barack Obama, celebrated basketball player Michael Jordan, media guru Oprah Winfrey, or international businesswoman Sara Treleaven Blakely. These people have one thing in common—they discovered something they were good at, invested all their resources in that one thing and today they are recognized all over the world for that one thing. It is this one engagement they have that opened the doors for other opportunities they enjoy today.

Sincerely, finding that one thing is not an easy feat. For instance, you and I may have to read books, attend conferences and workshops, beg a pastor to lay hands and legs on us, or get a degree that we will probably not use, before we finally discover that "one thing" we should focus all our energy, time, and resources on. We may have to engage in different activities until we experience an internal knowing about what our life's assignment should be. If we read life manuals like *Stay in Your Lane*, we have a higher chance of success by cutting the journey in half and avoiding the time wasters.

To gain this level of clarity and conviction, some people can push themselves (I call them self-motivated), while others will wait to be pushed. If you or someone you know falls into the category of people who will wait till someone pushes them, *Stay in Your Lane* is for you or that person. It pains me to see people live below their full potential. If you are a 10/10 person, you should play at the level of 10/10 and nothing less. If you are a 6/10 person, you should play at the level of 6/10 and nothing less. If you are a 4/10 person and you are living at 4/10 capacity, don't be intimidated by a 10/10 person. In the eyes of your creator and the world, you are both giving life your best.

We do not all have the same capacity to complete various projects. However, many people still struggle with the idea that potential is subject to their capacity. In the same way that purpose is unique to everyone, so is capacity (i.e., the skills, talents, and experiences needed to fulfill your life).

Let me break it down for you, if you can be 10/10 as a comedian and 5/10 as a college professor, then living as a fulltime comedian is living to your full potential. However, you could live at the average level as a college professor. Now the question is: Do you want to be a person working multiple jobs and not making a generational impact? Or do you want to be a person with one job, who is making a maximum impact and eventually creates a further impact on multiple works of life?

In my journey towards self-actualization, I have learned that I have the skills and natural inclinations to make me a good college professor. However, with the right simulation, I can also just as easily make people laugh, perhaps "at"the level of being a comedian if I apply myself properly. (Don't look so surprised, I can write jokes very easily, though sadly, I am yet to master the act of delivering jokes excellently). What I want you to take away from this is: will I be able to switch from a possible career in comedy (my mediocre lane) to a lane where my gifts and experiences are more at par (my exceptional lane)? This is a question only time can answer.

Many people think life is like a game of puzzle. They rush to put the pieces of the puzzle together, wrongly assuming that there are no specific questions that require specific answers. Other people go through life feeling like they are the right piece in the wrong puzzle. The pressure to have our lives figured out can lead to a series of frustrations. On the flip side, there are excellent examples of people who are sure of their specific destination. These people are doing well by staying in the lane of their giftings and talents. For example, Michael Jordan played professional basketball for 14 years but made most of his wealth from product endorsements and personal appearances. He was able to achieve this because he discovered he could play basketball better than engaging in other activities.

Another example is the late Steve Jobs. The bulk of Steve Jobs' wealth is from selling Pixar to Disney, but he is best known as the former CEO of Apple. That was because he saw a need for mobile phone technology, and he tried to meet the need.

Furthermore, consider Sara Treleaven Blakely. Blakely is an American billionaire, businesswoman, and founder of Spanx. Spanx is an American intimate apparel company founded in Atlanta, Georgia. In 2012, Blakely was named 1 of the 100 most influential people in the world in *Time* magazine's annual life, "Time 100." In 2019, at 48 years old, her net worth was 1.1 billion USD. Incredible!

This finally brings me to Oprah Winfrey. At the beginning of her television career, Oprah was demoted from the news division to a talk show because she was considered to be too emotional. The emotions they considered as a disadvantage, became an asset on the talk show, enabling her to connect with her listeners on multiple platforms. For example, the Oprah Winfrey Network (OWN).

Think about it. How do some people discover themselves early in life while others can barely remember their names as an adult? Marsai Martin is an American actress and producer, as well as an example of someone who discovered herself early in life – a young achiever.

She is known for her role as Diane Johnson in the ABC comedy series, *Black-ish*. She has further starred in the 2019 Universal Pictures comedy film *Little*, for which she was also an executive producer. At the age of 10, Martin pitched the idea for the film *Little* as modern spin on the film *Big*, to Universal Pictures. Martini started acting before she could talk as her parents enrolled her in Cathryn Sullivan Acting for Film school because they observed her talent for acting. At this very young age, she landed her first commercial with the Kim Dawson Agency and was able to secure a national campaign with Meineke.

As humans, we will always have a choice between the right thing and the fun thing. Unfortunately, some fun things have the potential to derail us from our destined path or lane. In the words of George Strait, "Life is not the breaths you take but the moments that take your breath away."

I have given the examples above to lead you to this conclusion. Since we have a limited time on the earth, it is crucial that we know our path , in order for us to reach our destination. We all have an inner compass, a GPS our creator put inside us for guidance on the journey, but it is our responsibility to be attuned with this compass and follow its directions. If we keep making the wrong turns, our destination and inherent GPS do not change; it just takes longer to get to our destination. When it takes an unnecessarily long time to see the fruits of their hard work, most people jump to the conclusion that they do not have the gifts, talents or passions for anything. This is not true. The problem is not a lack of gifts, talents or passions, but rather a lack of awareness of their originally intended journey.

In the chapters that follow, I will talk about people at different points in their self-discovery journey. The more you interact with these people, the more you will understand the importance of staying in your lane and working towards your own purpose. These categories of people are as follows:

1. People who don't know there is a destination in life.
2. People who don't know who they are or what they want.
3. People who don't know how to get to their destination.
4. People who don't know when they are in another person's lane.
5. People who are too shy to switch from another person's lane into their own lane because of public opinion and ridicule.
6. People who have been successful with what they do by staying in their lane.

PART 1

CHAPTER I

The Walking Blind:

People Who Don't Know There Is a Destination in Life

Everyone has a destination in life and your destination is specific to you. It is your responsibility to know your destination. How many people leave their house in the morning without having a destination? Could you imagine if you got into your car and just drove for hours in the direction of the wind? That would be a waste of gas and more importantly, a waste of time. This is the same reason you will not call your friend or a family member early in the morning and drive to their destination aimlessly.

Our strengths, weaknesses, resources, and challenges are all indication of our life's journey and destination. It is the culmination of these experiences that prepare us for our destination. What we are currently going through are preparations for what we are eventually supposed to do. My mum often used to say, a person who is going to be tall will initially have a deformed leg and many people will laugh at the person in the beginning. This undeniably correlated to the story of my youth. During my high school days at African Church Grammar School, I made friends with the best brains, but I could not achieve the level of success I desired because I kept myself away from other students. Later, I discovered that every person brings something new and useful to the table that everyone else cannot bring. We are all unique in our own way.

My academic path was rough during my undergraduate days at Obafemi Awolowo University, Nigeria. Before I started my undergraduate program, I had to sleep on the floor even though I could afford a better sleeping arrangement. I saved the money instead and invested it in any way I could. After I started my undergraduate program, my living environment was so poor that I found it difficult to study for my exams and quizzes. Additionally, at some point in my undergraduate studies, I tried all I could to gain admission to study medicine in a Nigerian university. I took the entry exam of Nigerian universities, the Joint Admission and Matriculation Board (JAMB) many times, but my cut off was still below the required score for medical students. There was an instance that I almost got accepted. Many people thought I got the admission. I decided to say nothing about it for a long time because of fear of what people would say. I used money for my supposed medical school expenses to buy shares in banks and other organizations I considered profitable. Despite my relatively high score on the Nigerian University JAMB entry exam, I eventually ended up studying Agriculture (animal sciences) as one of the candidates on a shortfall list. I went on to receive my bachelor's degree in Agriculture, then my master's degree in Biology. I just completed my Ph.D. in Integrated Biology at Florida Atlantic University, while teaching anatomy and physiology laboratories.

Although I did not end up becoming a medical doctor, I am in my natural habitat as a researcher and college professor. This is not to say that your initially desired career path is out of reach if you encounter some setbacks, remember my journey is unique to me. You must ask yourself why you want to achieve what you want, then drown the voices of impossibility.

If people tell you that your dreams are not possible, don't lose heart. It means you may have come up with a new idea. Generally, new things make people uncomfortable and they therefore write it off. So that seemingly impossible dream or idea might be what your destination or lane is. My dad is fond of saying this: you are the architect of your own fortune. I did not understand then when I was much younger, but I understand it now. I can decide to engage in something I will struggle with for the rest of my life, or I can engage in something that seems unfamiliar, but it is ultimately what I am meant to do. One way I think about this is discovering my WHY and my WHAT. For example, my WHY is to inspire people to be the best version of themselves. My WHAT is writing, teaching, training, researching, speaking, mentoring, motivating, and comedy. I am prepared to give the world an offer it cannot resist by using my talents and allowing these talents to open doors for me. Are you ready to do the same?

Nobody can know for you or transfer their experiences to you. That is why your journey through life and your destination is peculiar to you. If the journey is not clear in your own mind, then it will not be physically clear either. The purest and highest expression of yourself as a human is the path you should follow. You need to ask yourself, what do I really want? What do I have to offer?

Action Points:

1. Write down the names of your closest high school friends. How many of you in that group have the same work /careers now? What is the cause of the differences in the current path?
2. Contact these friends and ask them the same questions.
3. Check to see if your answers are similar to theirs.

CHAPTER 2

The Uncertain Crowd:

People Who Don't Know Who They Are or What They Want

The journey toward your life's potential involves people. Our relationships often reflect our ability to adapt to tough and conflicting situations. This is why I have always invested in the relationships with my young proteges. It's not uncommon to find men and women entering the dating world without a clear understanding of who they are or where they are heading in life. Let me ask you the following questions: Can you make friends with yourself? Can you be a friend to the person in the mirror? If you are uncertain about your answers to these questions, it is because you are a stranger to yourself. You must get to know who you are. Like the saying goes: Take yourself out, date yourself and do you. You should engage in activities that will make you become more aware of yourself. You can engage in activities like traveling. Traveling to a new place allows you to learn about other people's cultures. You could also take a class on an extracurricular activity or subject that you find interesting - if you like singing or playing a musical instrument, you could enroll in music lessons.

Let's detour a little and talk about relationships. The reason many people struggle with dating is because they did not date themselves first. We often think about dating as a means to curb loneliness. In this case, it amounts to giving a toy to a baby and hoping he or she will stop crying. Sometimes the baby will go to sleep; sometimes that toy is the reason the baby will not sleep. Dating is an emotional gamble. Some people become poor because of it; others become rich because of it. Some people end up with the right person through dating and others end up with the wrong person because of dating. Sometimes dating works and sometimes it does not. The whole point is, if you believe in it then you should give it a try with a clear and common intentions, as well as an open mind.

When I was in a purposeful relationship during my younger years, things did not go my way (marriage). During my days in the National Youth Service Corps (NYSC) (A program designed by the Nigerian government to get Nigerian graduates involved in building and developing the country) I had a friend who contested for the Miss NYSC competition. I supported her and she became the first runner-up for the most beautiful girl in the Miss NYSC competition. I was redeployed from my initial posting and, as a result, we could no longer see each other every day. She became very upset by this and the relationship ended when she became unresponsive to my efforts. However, we were on good terms. Based on this experience, as well as others, I came to the conclusion that friendship is more important than dating. Finding someone that shares the same values as you, is ultimately more important than random dating. I call this value sharing rather than dating. I would like to note, however, that value sharing is not the same as what some people call "friends with benefits."

Regardless of how good you are with dating; you cannot sing your way into love like Brandy and Monica. You must be intentional and strategic. I was never really the ladies' man, but I will share with you what I learned.

Ask for her name. Show that you care and find common ground. I started working as program coordinator with the Graduate Professional Student Association, Florida Atlantic University (FAU), I later got promoted to an assistant director position with GPSA, FAU. While at work I met a fellow graduate student. I asked for her name. I empathized with her and showed that I cared by giving her suggestions on how to get a job. When her other options failed, I helped her get a job as a program coordinator with GPSA, FAU, the position I had previously. We were friends for some time. I was struck by cupid, and I decided to ask her out on a date. I utilized the popular question that Americans tend to ask every time, "do you want to grab a cup of coffee or go to the beach?"

My relationship with my friend blossomed because I discovered in good time that one person is always right in a relationship and in my relationship, that person was not me. I stole my girlfriend's heart, and she took my last name as an act of revenge. Marriage: a fancy word for adopting an overgrown male child who can no longer be handled by his parents anymore. How did I know this? I studied all through the night after my wedding and while we were courting. I discovered that I can pray some of my problems away from marriage, but I cannot pray disagreements away. After arguing with my wife, she would ask me to sleep on the couch. I became convinced that she did not understand the mess she got into when she married a culturally inclined African man with a thick Nigerian accent, and, to prevent my wife from saying she does not need me, I would spend the last minutes of most arguments tightening all the bottled jars in the house.

For you, if you want to get a lady's attention, apologize to her for no reason because even wicked ladies like overly courteous guys. If she asks you why you are sorry, tell her you are sorry because she doesn't know why you are sorry. Do all you can: offer her a Ph.D., slide into her direct messages unknowingly. If she asks you why, tell her it is because the ground is slippery, remove the "sir stigma" as quickly as possible. It is difficult for men to ask women out if the "sir stigma" is there, do not pick your nose when you are on a date, make sure your grammar is not too bombastic to the extent that your date needs gallons of water to swallow your words.

The more stories you have in common with her on the first date, the more likely you will have the opportunity of a second date. Finding common ground is the most difficult part of the first date. Most men lie about having something in common with a woman for obvious reasons on the first date. Think about it, women fall in love with what they hear, men fall in love with what they see, and therefore women wear makeup and men lie in some cases. We are both guilty of the crime of misleading our love interests. On a more serious note, honesty is the best policy. Stay away from lies as much as possible. Good ladies and women prefer honesty. Do not give up on love, hang around the barbershop long enough to receive a haircut that will make your crush accept your love proposal. If you cannot find the right partner, simply move the left to the right if you have what it takes. The problem is that you cannot give what you do not have to your love interests, smart people know this. For example, when you try to talk to ladies, the first thing they do is look at your shoes. They know you cannot give what you do not have. My advice to young people in the dating world is this: Before you attempt to know or be known by another, you should get to know yourself first. Can you write a full page of paper on yourself in two minutes? If your answer is yes, then you might have a good idea of who you are.

We all need to work with other people to achieve our full potential. Go out of your way to have conversations with people that are very different from you (for example, people who don't share the same beliefs with you). This simple exercise will expand your views about life, and you will consequently discover something new about yourself and others. People who don't share the same beliefs with you. This exercise will expand your view about life, and you will consequently discover something new about yourself.

Another way to discover a sense of who you are is to reflect on your childhood experiences and see if there is a pattern that can guide you. As a child, I was the slowest and most awkward of my parents' five children. I remember not being able to read two- or three-letter words in the brighter grammar book (a book on introduction to English language for kids). Reading sentences was almost impossible for me. Despite my earlier challenges with reading, I am the first in the family to receive an American degree, Ph.D., and write a book.

This goes to say that you should not write yourself off based on your background or the limitations encountered in the past. There are opportunities in every crisis and there is a path to follow in order to seize the opportunities. Our pain is a preparation for our ordained destination.

Apart from having strong and successful relationships, we can also discover our life's destination by adequately deploying our gifts. Consider Michael Jr., the popular comedian, for instance. He could not read two syllables when he was young. He had to see words in seven different ways before he could pronounce them. Today, he uses the skill that at first appeared to be a disadvantage (seeing things from seven different ways), as a tool for his comedy. He was preparing for his destiny during his younger days, even though others may have believed that he was merely disabled.

Discover your gifts and your gifts will make a path for you. You may wonder, how do I discover my gifts? Well, think about what you do so easily, perhaps when you are playing around, which other people consider great. That will give you an inkling of your gifts because your gifts are the common things you do that people believe you are doing in an exceptionally excellent way. What are these things in your case? However, it is important to note that a gift is not measured by how much someone else likes or praises you, but rather by how much someone else needs it. If you are not using your gift, you are wasting your time and hindering the destiny of others (A good number of people might have to use the light from your lane to illuminate their lane). Think about how not living your full capacity may allow other people live a wasted life.

When you share your talents, you have room to receive more. If you give what you think are your talents, two things can happen;

you can become better at it or you can discover something else you want to eventually get better at. This is a win-win situation for you. To illustrate this point, I was asked to facilitate our Christmas brunch at the Church I attended. This was a way for me to evaluate whether I am good at facilitating events or not. When I was done, a man at my table specially thanked me for being brief and concise with the relevant questions I asked to facilitate the discussion at my table. Also, my questions made the conversations very interesting to most people at the table. What a timely compliment! At another instance, I gave a humorous speech at the public speaking and leadership club I attend (Toastmasters international). During this speech I sang for 15 seconds and some of the individuals in the audience thought I sang well. A member from the audience joked that I might have missed my calling as a singer. After that experience, I decided to take singing and playing instruments more seriously. Now, I play my guitar regularly and I just bought a piano. Our gifts are like the little muscles we all have that, when exercised, become bigger. Most of us just expect the "talent muscle" to miraculously become bigger without exercising our gifts. We all need a space to grow in our talents and gifts. For most people this space is a church, volunteer organization, or nonprofit organization. When I was trying to confirm my area of influence through leadership and communication, I organized free masterminds in my Church and Florida Atlantic University.

When you discover your gifts, you will live your life with conviction, until then, you may find that you are restless. But in order to discover your gift, you must keep searching and you must try new things. You will never fail at discovering yourself, until you stop trying new things. This is why I often become sad when I meet people who do not have excitement or a desire to try new things. The journey of self-discovery is a continuous one. It is not always about asking if we did something wrong, but it is also about asking if we eventually did something right. The effort to reflect on this is immeasurably valuable as certificates and degrees cannot give us the blessings that our talents and gifts can offer us.

Now, let me address one gift that is common to all of us- Time. One day our time on earth will come to an end, and we will be asked to give an account of how we invested the gift of time that was so generously given to us. Spend time to know yourself. Spend time doing productive things. Spend time learning. Remember, you only live once, so use your time well.

Now, let me circle back to how I started this chapter, which is the importance of getting to know yourself. I performed exercises that made me more in touch with my reality and therefore, I discovered things about myself that still serve me today. For instance, I was able to discover that I think better when I am walking than when I am sitting. Therefore, I write better typing on my phone while walking in a safe area. I also discovered that I like celebrating - Give me a reason to celebrate and I will celebrate regardless of how small the achievement is in other people's eyes. I do not believe that you need a big achievement to celebrate and people like me are often referred to as "happy people".

My care for other people makes me likable. It is a blessing to have such a personality trait. I use it to my advantage. I am real, genuine, and easy to get along with. Although my wife says I overdo it sometimes, I have an immense care for other people. What I like about myself is what some people don't like about me (i.e., likeability). Some people think that likeability place you all over the place with less solid personality. What do you think?

Get married to yourself before you get married to someone else. You can't control how the world treats you, but you can control how you treat and love yourself. Although love shatters reasoning and defies logic, we must start with and practice self-love.

To know who you are, take yourself on a date. Know your abilities, limitations, potential, and the resources that are at your disposal. You can also get to know yourselves by taking the calculated risk of engaging in new activities. If you can perform that new activity very well, then focus on honing that skill. You have every reason to believe you can do well. Make it your duty to overcome the fear of possible failure. Remember that the feeling of failure is better than the feeling of regret. Take actions based on self-awareness, the way you think, the things you like, and the things that keep you inspired.

I also learned about creative spaces. We all have different creative spaces. Some people become creative when they are watching a soccer game while others become creative when they are in the gym. Personally, my creative space is the bathroom when I am taking my shower. I have always viewed taking a shower as a form of therapy because my creativity flourishes under the shower; All sorts of productive ideas come to me when I am showering. Funny enough, my sacred time showering has caused me to have problems. When I first had to share a bathroom with a female, she was not happy about the long time I spent in the bathroom showering. She would knock on the door of the bathroom and rain abusive words on me, which caused me to feel embarrassed.

Jokes apart, keep in mind that "success is who you are." Do not try to be like anyone else. Stay on course and be patient. You must know what you cannot do in order to know what you can do. For instance, I once tried being a Forex trader prematurely and, unsurprisingly, that did not work out. Now, I am back to learning Forex. People rewrite long bad stories to good ones in order to receive more appreciation and enjoyment. People telling you "no" can be a gift that allows you to eventually receive the yes you need.

All I've known in the last ten years of my life is studying; sitting in front of a laptop writing, reading, and doing research. Nobody can really make a generational impact by sitting in front of a laptop unless they are solving real-world problems (Ex. solving problems for a multinational company or keeping people safe during a pandemic like COVID-19).

It is important to pay attention to all the emotional cycles you go through every day. These emotions can indicate what you should devote the rest of your life to. Struggling makes us discover our inner strengths that we previously did not know we had. Your talent or gift is what is leftover when the love for a particular activity fades away.

What do most people like to do but you do not like to do? Or what do most people not like to do but you like to do? Most people are trying to figure out their WHAT. But what they should really do is to figure out their WHY. However, you cannot know your WHAT and WHY unless you know your WHO. Your WHO is the door to your WHY and your WHY is a door to your WHAT. Your WHAT is obvious to everyone and that is what people see clearly. But they still wonder what your WHY is because of the way you conduct your life. In most cases nobody knows your WHY if you don't clearly state it. For example, I walk around my apartment every night and most of my neighbors ask why I do this. During this COVID-19 period, I spend my days sitting down to teach, read, conduct research, and write; The only way I stay sane for the remaining part of the day, and keep in shape, is by taking a walk at night or riding my bicycle.

Have the courage to live a life that is true to yourself and not the life others expect you to live. You can't be happy with anything you do until you are happy with yourself. Who you are is your greatest strength and your signature. Be different from the crowd and ensure that you do things in a unique manner. Bring something to the table that nobody else can bring. Always leverage your uniqueness in every situation and use it as your selling point. Don't act like everyone else. Find something that you do well and do it as if your existence depends on it. People might say you are too serious. However, they will always come back to thank you for your seriousness. I have experienced this with my students. I am approachable and friendly. But when it is time to work, my students and co-workers often say that I am too serious. As a child, my dad used to encourage me to work hard and after a lot of his stories, he would end the discussion by saying, "*E we ke yon koin*" (a proverb in Yoruba that means to "work harder than anybody you know around you") that is the secret to success.

Open your mouth and sing your songs of praise; Nobody can sing your songs the way you can sing them. Learn to say no and stop letting other people tell you who you are! Success is who you are. Normal is overrated...you must be unapologetically you!

A lot of people leave their mask on; they are not what they were created to be, but are what others want them to be. Take your mask off so you can see your lane clearly and stay in it.

What have you learned recently that changed the way you live? What do you love most about yourself?

Action Points:

1. What hobby do you find yourself engaging in frequently even though you're tired and unpaid for doing it?
2. Write a full page about yourself in two minutes. Ask five of your closest friends to each write a page about you in two minutes. Compare what you wrote with what your friends wrote. The time limit will ensure that they are not being partial in their descriptions.

CHAPTER 3

The Lost Travelers

People Who Don't Know How to Get to Their Destination

The lost Travelers have witnessed other people reach their potential. They have watched their friends, mentors, and colleagues reached their maximum capacity, but they just don't know how to go about their personal journey. They might have even helped other people reach their destination knowingly or unknowingly. They might be a pastor, a boss or a confidant. They don't have a map or GPS. My recommendation for this group is this: You can start by talking to people who have done what you are planning to do, and even take it a step further by asking if they can mentor you in this area.

We cannot become what we want by remaining who we are. We must keep moving regardless of the obstacle we face. There are societies and volunteer groups I belong to that have given me the opportunity to keep moving in my lane: The John Maxwell Team, Toastmasters International, Phi Kappa Phi, etc. I did basic and advanced leadership certifications at the Daystar Leadership Academy in Lagos, Nigeria, before I joined the John Maxwell Team to learn more about communication and leadership. I also discovered I needed to become better with my public speaking: I joined Toastmasters International to help with the delivery of my speech. I now know I am not supposed to say "er," "um," "so," and other "crutch words" while speaking as they are distracting, and people do not like them. I learned that I should pause and say things as clearly as possible. I have been using John Maxwell Team content and other resources to improve my teaching. I decided it is time for me to write down my own content for teaching and training purposes. I decided to write part of my experiences in the form of this book (*Stay in Your Lane*). It feels good to know that I can give my grandkids my book to read, so that I can watch TV. Think of it like using one stone to kill two birds.

If you are lost on which direction to go, why not get some training in your areas of interest? Think about a group that can offer you valuable information or a volunteering opportunity in your area of interest. My friend's daughter, who is studying the sciences, needed guidance on how she should navigate her career. Her problem is that she does not like chemistry, mathematics, and biology. However, she likes the physiological aspects of biology. She is also thinking of studying political science, despite her passion for music. My advice to her was to think about the areas of learning music that is coordinated with physiology of the body. For example, how the respiratory system helps to produce the right sound during singing. I also recommended that she learn an instrument. Perhaps you are in a similar situation, following a traditional career path while nursing interests in the more creative fields. Give yourself options. Follow your creative streak. Pick up a skill and hone it. If possible, find a way to make the two worlds intersect.

Action Points:

1. List five defining moments in your life.
2. List five of your core values (the most important ones).
3. List five types of the resources you have at your disposal.
4. Match your defining moment and your core values together. You may only match one item to another. Rank your match from first to fifth, based on the level of fulfillment in your heart when you think about engaging in them.
5. Start trying your options from the first. If the first doesn't work, go to the second. Continue in this manner until you reach the fifth on your ranking list. If you reach an obstacle based on the resources you do not have, think about an alternative resource that will work.

CHAPTER 4

The Lane Jumpers

People Who Don't Know When They Are in Another Person's Lane

People in this category do not follow protocol. Some people even pay money to boycott rules and regulations, thereby attracting the bad will and wrath of the less privileged. This is a common occurrence in developing countries like Nigeria, where the elite can decide to show off their wealth in a disgusting manner. However, when people who engage in this act (the elite and the common people) run into a ditch, they blame it on the society and deities based on superstitious beliefs.

Speaking of religious superstitions, there are people who believe that the only reason they are not living the life of their dreams is because they have not destroyed their enemies with prayers. Not every problem is a result of demonic influence. Rather than blame imagined enemies for your woes, why not ask yourself when was the last time you gained new knowledge in your area of influence, or the new venture you are planning to pursue? Most of the destiny accidents (failures and regrets) happen when the person is not equipped for an endeavor, instead, decides to follow a certain path just because people recommended this path. It is your responsibility to gain the adequate knowledge and skills before starting your journey into the new business.

It's hard for these people to see that they are wearing another person's shoes, that is, pursuing another person's dreams. How many of you have worn an oversized shoe when you were young? How far were you able to walk in an oversized shoe? Did you walk in a straight line? Or a pattern safe enough to call your lane?

Typically, it takes three to five years for most people to become highly skilled in a new field. If you have been engaging in an area of work for more than five years and you cannot see that you have made clear progress, then maybe it is time to switch lanes. Do not try to engage in multiple passions, in such a manner that the development of one passion is hindering the development of the other passions. You should focus on the few areas that are your strengths. Find one thing and pour yourself into it. That is what will give you the returns that you deserve.

Action Points:

1. Write down the business your friends, family or neighbors engage in.
2. Write five reasons you find your friends', family's or neighbor's business more profitable than your own business. What are the things that will matter to you five to twenty years from now? Which of the reasons you wrote down in 2a can help you achieve the things that will matter to you between five to twenty years from now?
3. Write out ten people that you think truly love you.
4. Of these ten people, which one of them will not create adequate time for you? Remove them from the list. Of the

remaining number, how many will be willing to give you feedback from the action points in Chapter 3 and Chapter 4? You should talk to them immediately.

CHAPTER 5

The Obsessive Thinkers

People Who Worry About What Other People Think

There are certain categories of people who do not like to be embarrassed; they will do everything within their power to avoid failure. These people prefer to be miserable rather than risk potential embarrassment. Fear has taken control of their lives. These groups consist of people that are too afraid to call a spade a spade. They can call a spade a spoon just so they can get away with a comfortable and easy life. These people prefer not to see situations the way they really are because of fear. The fear of people's opinion is a real crippling factor in the pursuit of their purpose. A lot of people are afraid of what people will think of them, so much so that they leave their lane and move to someone else's lane, simply because it seems more appealing.

Action Points:

1. List the resources you need to switch to a new lane.
2. List where to find the resources.
3. Take the first step to reach out to the person who has the resources you need today. Send the email, make the call, take a drive down or talk to someone who knows someone in possession of the resources you need.

4. Make bold statements to your friends and family on your next business or idea adventure. Encourage your family and friends to hold you accountable for everything you said.

CHAPTER 6

The Life Hackers

People Who Have Been Successful with What They Do by Staying in Their Lane

Have you ever turned on the TV and watched someone who is successful in their field? If you have, have you ever wondered how the person did it? How was this person able to achieve so much success? Whether it is in sports, politics, or entertainment, there are people who have successfully dominated their field. I see and read about some of these people and I simply marvel. As someone who enjoys speaking publicly there are a handful of people who come to mind as some of the greatest public speakers of our time, one of these speakers is Martin Luther King Jr.

Some may say that Martin Luther King Jr. had a calling to speak in front of thousands of people. A calling can be described as a predestined role in life that you were made for. However, even if Martin Luther King had this calling, he still needed practice and experience in order to become what he was called to do. Just from reading his work and studying his legacy, I learned that even as a young boy, Martin Luther King Jr. spoke at events held in his church and school. King's very first public speech, at seventeen years old, was at Ebenezer Baptist Church, where his father was a pastor. At this church, he developed the skills and confidence to speak in front of others. We all know and learned about Martin Luther King Jr.'s famous "I Have a Dream" speech that he proclaimed on the steps of the Lincoln Memorial. Sometimes our road to success begins at an early age. Try to think of something you were known to be good at while you were younger. For me, when I was younger, most of my family enjoyed my funny and positive approach to life. No matter how bad a situation looked, there was always a reason to laugh or crack a joke in order to make other people feel relaxed.

What you were meant to do can also be something that has been part of your family's legacy. Some of us try to run away from becoming like our parents, or grandparents. In some cases, we should, but sometimes the things our parents did can be looked at as more of a starting point of our journey. My mum, who is a pastor, used to say that all her kids would become pastors. What an expensive joke! As of today, none of us is a pastor. But there are a few of us that engage in speaking roles at different levels. Who knows, maybe one day one of us will become a pastor? That person is probably not me. My point is: nothing is impossible. I believe a good start for any profession is having excellent communication skills. I remember telling my wife that I'd want our daughters to follow their own passions, they do not have to go deep into academia and get a PhD like I did, but if my daughters choose to follow in our footsteps, then I would encourage them to make it their own. Their path must completely be their choice.

Another person who is staying in his lane is Aliko Dangote. Aliko Dangote is known as the richest person in Africa. He has accumulated his wealth through his many business ventures as the CEO of Dangote Group. His great grandfather from his mother side, Alhassan Dantata was also once known as the richest person in West Africa. Alhassan Dantata made a lot of money from selling nuts (kola nuts and groundnuts). His grandfather Sanusi Dantata was also a successful entrepreneur. Although Dangote came from a family of successful entrepreneurs, he was able to develop his own personal love and skills in the trading and the entrepreneurial world.

It is important to mention that not everyone is going to know exactly what they are meant to do early on in life. Some will discover themselves quite late in life. The goal is to find the lane that has your name written on it and to stay there. Jeff Bezos, Amazon CEO, did not start at Amazon. Jeff Bezos was like many of us because he took many turns to finally get to his destination. Jeff Bezos was born in Albuquerque and raised in Houston, then later Miami. Bezos graduated from Princeton University in 1986. Bezos holds a degree in Electrical Engineering and Computer Science. All along Jeff Bezos knew that the opportunities the internet can offer has not been fully exploited. He had a passion for customer satisfaction in entrepreneurship while he was working on Wall Street, in a variety of related fields from 1986 to early 1994. Bezos eventually followed his passion, he founded Amazon in late 1994 while on a cross-country road trip from New York City to Seattle. The company began as an online bookstore and has since expanded to a wide variety of other e-commerce products and services, including video and audio streaming, cloud computing, and artificial intelligence. Amazon is currently the world's largest online sales company, the largest Internet company by revenue, and the world's largest provider of virtual assistants and cloud infrastructure services through its Amazon Web Services branch.

Staying in your lane does not mean you will never face obstacles. The successful people we see today were able to stay in their lane despite the challenges they faced. One person who also readily comes to mind is the comedian, Steve Harvey. Before Steve Harvey was known for hosting shows on daytime TV and becoming a New York Times best seller, he was a struggling stand-up comedian. He once shared a story about how he was able to land the gig hosting the Apollo comedy club. Not having any money, Harvey was asked to fly to New York from Florida to appear on the Apollo stage on a Sunday night. Just as he was feeling hopeless and trying to figure out how he was going to get enough money to fly to New York, a friend called him and asked if he wanted to make $150 by performing at a comedy club that Friday night. Steve Harvey was able to make it to the comedy club and ended up making $300 by performing both Friday and Saturday night of that weekend. He made it to the Apollo that Sunday night, and his performance signaled the start of his success. Keep moving in your lane and God will make a way.

Staying in your lane does not mean you should never evolve. Everyone that I have mentioned in this chapter have evolved in one way or another to become the best version of themselves. They might have written books, started a new business adventure, or pursued other passions. The one thing that each one of these successful people were able to do is master their talent and use it as the core for every other things they were able to do. For example, John Maxwell. Many people know him as a pastor, author, leadership guru, and professional speaker. John Maxwell at his core is a public speaking guru. Whether he is speaking one-on-one or speaking to an audience of thousands, he can connect with his audience easily.

Action Points:

1. List the names of the successful people you know who stayed in a particular lane and refused to give up. How many of these people are in the same area of field you are interested in? Do you know anyone that knows these persons personally?

2. Reach out to the individuals that know these successful people personally, so that the individuals can connect you with the successful people.

3. When you meet these successful people, do not ask them for money; ask them to mentor you in the area you believe is your area of influence.

PART TWO

Now that we've looked at the six lanes, the next part of the book is directed to help you understand the inhibitions that can keep you from staying in your lanes and fulfilling your potential. We will begin with fear.

CHAPTER 7

Fear

There is a common nugget of wisdom which says that we learn from our mistakes. However, if we learn from our mistakes, why are we always so afraid to make mistakes? The answer is fear. Fear of what people will say has crippled so many and prevented them from making progress. I touched on this earlier on in the book and I will make it more in-depth in this chapter. Fearful people often would rather be content with misery than to risk embarrassment. I remember when my high school Chemistry teacher, Mr. Sofela, explained that there is no reason to be fearful of answering Chemistry questions incorrectly because other students might stare at you. "Even if they stare at you," he said, "they will have to eventually take their eyes off because if they do not take their eyes away, that means there is a problem, and the Chemistry lesson will stop."

If life is so short, why do we do so many things we do not like and like so many things we don't do? The answer is once again fear. Like an unknown person paraphrased, FEAR can be considered an acronym for: "False Evidence Appearing Real." We should all understand that the regret from failure is better than regret from not trying. If you place regret from not trying and fear of failure on a scale, fear of failure will weigh less. This is why people with fear feel less burden than people who have regrets from not trying a new thing. Try the new idea you have on your mind. What if you do not fail?

Most of the things that I feared did not happen to me. I feared that:

1. I would wake up one day without legs. I still have my legs.
2. I would be kicked out of my PhD program. I just completed my PhD.
3. I would not have good people around me. Today I have countless good people around me.
4. I would not have money to do good things in life. I am doing well financially.
5. I would not get married. I am married to my loving wife with two beautiful daughters.

Although my fears are seemingly mundane, they were genuine and could easily have crippled me from pursuing my goals. However, there are people with more challenging situations; People who inherited their fears. Some people call it generational curses because they find it difficult to wrap their minds around the situation. Let me point out that although people sometimes mix up the two, fear is different from generational curses. Now, you may wonder: How do you respond to people whose fears have a psychological background? The people who inherit their fears. Remember, to these people, fears are like sociological constraints. These are extreme fears that appear to be more real than the fears we experience every day. For example, the fear that you will die from a disease that killed one of your family members. This fear is usually the case for terminal diseases like cancer. How do such people have a chance with navigating the issues of life?

One way of dealing with such salient fears is by developing and maintaining an intentional support system.

On the other hand, there are people who are not supportive, no matter what you need or what you are going through, they simply cannot be there for you. How do you deal with these naysayers? Again, I will remind you that everybody will give an account of their life. Encourage the person to understand your perspective on the situation and be willing to listen to their own suggestions. People can modify your journey through life because they have greater wisdom due to their experiences. However, they should not stop you from what you are predestined to do.

Don't be intimidated by what you don't know. There is a reason you have the fear. You take a fear of flying class and still always miss the class, because you are busy flying already. What a funny situation! Fear does not make any sense, if you think about it very well. We are fearful because of how we spend our time, without realizing that it's more important to be with our family and friends: Before we know the most precious resources we have, time is gone. We don't have the luxury of time, but we have the luxury of living life to our full capacity.

What you did by mistake becomes part of your experience, even if it is a mistake you will laugh about it in old age. I don't regret my failures. I feel cool and courageous about my past failures. I laugh at myself when I remember my failures. Success can be overrated, anyway. It makes people think it is their birthright to always succeed or win. Therefore, they look down on others that appear to be struggling with failure. Whenever I fail, I remind myself that at least I tried. I look around and I see people who are not willing to try. Then, I focus on the lessons from my failure so that I do not repeat the same mistake again.

I was very introverted, especially when it came to women. I later discovered that with women the worst feeling was not actually hearing "NO", but instead, having the guts to walk up to a woman without knowing how she felt about me. I would rather deal with a "NO" from any request than have the regret of not trying or asking. When I first came to America, I had a female friend who was also from one of the African countries. At the time, like most students, I struggled financially. Sometimes I would hardly have any food to eat. I would often queue in a long line to get free food at events that my university hosted. The relationship with my working-class female friend whom I liked, and I thought she liked me too is a very good example of what fear can do. I attempted to get closer to her, and ask if she wanted to hang out, she would immediately put up a defense by claiming her schedule was too busy. Later when I got engaged and I went to her office to give her a letter of invitation to my wedding. She was so shocked by the news of my engagement that she almost passed out. I had to walk with her so that she could get some fresh air. She did not attend my wedding as I expected based on her response to my engagement, instead she explained why she could not attend. My point is, if she did not hold herself back, perhaps things would have been different. Despite this, I have no regrets and I am married to a beautiful woman whom I love very much.

I had a similar experience with my high school crush. I felt my heart stopped beating when she was around me, (of course, thinking back now, that was ridiculous). On our way coming back from our after-school classes, she would wait for me to catch up with her. But while she was clearly waiting for me, I would pretend something fell from my hand onto the ground, and it took me all day to look for it. When she got tired and started moving, I would continue walking too. I clearly liked this lady, but I suppressed the emotions because I thought I was going to pass out if I talked to her.

As I got older, I decided to confront my fears about approaching women. I sat down at a bus stop and I made it a must to say hello to every single woman who passed by. I did not get any dates from these women, but I broke my fear. If you do not break your fears, your fears will break you. You must confront your fears. Fear is one of life's greatest time wasters. We have a limited amount of time on earth and we do not know how much time we have left. You should not live your life in a self-imposed prison. If you must live in a prison, at least make sure you did not construct the prison by yourself. Give other people the privilege of doing the construction work for you. Fear is a form of self-imposed prison. Fear leads to an unhappy, miserable, and isolated life. The strength to break your fears is within you. You need to reach out for it. You need to get to a point where you answer the call associated with the NIKE brand, "Just do it". Even if you fall, you can rise and try again. Do not stay on the ground.

I can talk about fears for weeks without stopping because I have too many firsthand experiences. For instance, many people do not know that I had a speech defect. I struggled with grammar and could not pronounce two-lettered words. One of my professors stated my English was so bad there was no way I could be a PhD student. Contrary to his/her expectation of me, I just completed my PhD. I have McKnight graduate fellowship, graduate fellowship for academic excellence, and other fellowships that supported my PhD program. However, I developed a level of fear like most people; I was ashamed to ask for help because I feared rejection. I narrowly missed the common postgraduate entry requirement and job entry requirement GPA in Nigeria because I was too embarrassed to make a simple request. I wanted to ask my department head to remove an elective course, which would have raised my GPA, but I was too afraid to ask. I later found out that one of my classmates, who made a similar request enjoyed the benefit I could not enjoy just because I failed to ask. Please ask and ask on time; this is one of the basic principles of life. Like the saying goes, "a closed mouth is a closed destiny".

I also experienced fear with my friend during my undergraduate degree. I feared getting her pregnant, which prevented me from having a real relationship with her. She wanted me to go to social gatherings with her, but I wouldn't allow that to happen because I was trying to keep my distance. Hence, we remain just being friends.

My beautiful wife switched lanes regardless of her fears. Her journey is a typical example of staying in the appropriate lane. People feel ashamed to leave a profession that they have been accustomed to for years because of what other people will say. My wife is a Certified Public Accountant (CPA), but she only practices part time. Even though she liked writing, everybody advised her to be an accountant because accountants make decent amount of money. She kept practicing accounting, but the passion to write remained. I encouraged her to start writing and supported her putting her accounting certifications on the back burner and following her passion for writing despite the financial disadvantage. I encouraged her to follow her passion and keep writing every day. I checked to see she accomplished something every day. Before long, her book, *Purposeful Choice Making for Teenagers and Young Adults*, was completed and released. She is currently working on her movie script. All throughout this time her friends were making a lot of money while she was busy attending online writing school. She left the lane that she was familiar with and she moved to a lane that she was predestined to be. She had an anxiety about passing the CPA exam, but when she is writing, she is free from anxiety or any other problem or fears she is facing.

My wife shared a story from one of her former colleagues who was also a CPA. He would come to the firm with delicious food and often said that he wanted to open his restaurant as his passion was to be a chef. My wife would ask, "why are you here?" and then ask herself why she was struggling to become a CPA when she was passionate about writing. She would encourage her co-worker to follow his dreams and become a chef. One of the major secrets of happiness is to live according to our values. Writing helped my wife with anxiety issues and consequently she is living according to her values. We all need to find our destined lane and stay in it!

My friend and accountability partner, Ozzie, was in a similar situation. He left his job as a sales representative to pursue his passion in line with professional speaking. He was doing well financially at his previous job and had a thriving career. The first day he attended a

Toastmasters meeting, he called his wife and told her that his life had been changed. He had never engaged in public speaking before, but after his first experience he felt speaking was something he was supposed to engage in for the rest of his life (this is his exceptional lane). He was convinced speaking was what he was supposed to do. His fears about providing for his family were genuine, but he did not allow that fear to deter him from making the necessary plans and taking the step that he needed to take, to have a career in his exceptional lane.

Like many in Ozzie's shoes, there are legitimate concerns such as financial responsibility for our families, which makes us believe that we do not have the freedom to follow our dreams. However, true freedom comes from your mind. You cannot control most of life's situations, (like losing a job or the company you work at is going bankrupt), but we can control our reactions and thoughts in our mind. Ozzie educated himself on finances to alleviate his concerns of him losing his job one day. He drew lessons from the book, *The Richest Man in Babylon,* by George S. Clason. Ozzie saved up enough money to cover rent for six to seven months, take care of his kids, and enough money for rainy days, like a day the car might break down. Even though he left his job, he left it with a solid plan- The goal in life is to take calculated risks.

I overcame my fear of being jobless after graduation from my first degree when I became the Assistant Manager at a catering outlet in Nigeria called "Mamacass Restaurant". I had gotten the job by approaching the Manager and telling her that I was a Youth Corper Member (a new graduate in Nigeria undergoing the National Youth Service Corps Program). I got the job after weeks of persistently asking the manager for weeks. No wonder people say that getting a job is a job. Life opens the door for us if we make a demand long enough.

In academia, there is a popular argument that extra credit is not good. Many people claim extra credit impedes the effort of hard-working students. In my earlier days of teaching, I was more hesitant about giving extra credits to my students. When I was considering which daycare is best for my daughter, I realized one of the caretakers in the daycare was my former student– Imagine my surprise! I immediately had a fearful thought; would she harm my daughter because I was not the most generous with grades? These fears were unfounded, and it turned out that she was quite excited that my wife and I were considering the daycare she worked at (we ended up choosing another option for reasons that were completely unrelated).

The thought of public speaking for the first time in toastmaster gave me nightmares and chills at the same time. After my first public speaking engagement, speaking became a lot easier. Now I have the confidence to compete in contests and win awards. Action reduces fear. Many of us are familiar with the phrase "courage does not mean the absence of fear." I like to think that courage means you are a master of your fears and no longer a slave to your fears. I had fears about getting married to my wife, an American lady because of differences in culture. Despite the cultural differences, we are still happily married today. I acted even in the face of fears. Acting in the face of fears is courageous. We all need to learn how to act courageously.

People told my wife: "don't date a guy whose mattress is on the floor; he is not ready for marriage." But my wife dated and married me despite my mattress being on the floor. Guess what? My mattress is no longer on the floor. People evolve over time, unless they do not put in the effort.

Action Points:

1. Pick up the phone and call that person you have always wanted to talk to. Send the mail, send the text, tell your boss how you feel about the new project. Ask your date about the goal of the relationship.
2. Let us see whether the world is going to end suddenly based on your actions.

CHAPTER 8

The Main Street Lights for Safety

The qualities you need on your journey to actualizing your full potential can be likened to streetlights on the highway. This is because, just like streetlights, these qualities equip you to see the road ahead. These qualities help you to stay in your lane and they ultimately prevent accidents (for example regrets and fears). Below I have briefly described some of the streetlights necessary for self-actualization:

1. Character
2. Self-Celebration
3. Communication Skills
4. Health Condition
5. Environment
6. State of Mind
7. Prejudice & Bias
8. Exposure
9. Gratitude
10. Generosity
11. Relationships
12. Leadership

13. Attitude

14. Service

15. Improvement

16. Adaptability

17. Exercise and Hygiene

18. Salesmanship

19. Showmanship

20. Self-belief

21. Culture

22. Responsibility

23. Sacrifice

24. Rest

25. Emotion

26. Entertainment

27. Education

28. Avoid Scamming

29. Values

30. People

31. Sexual Purity

32. Time

33. Memorability

34. Innovation

35. Feedback

36. Reflection

37. Reading

38. Writing

I would like to start with character because I believe that the beginning of every human achievement can be traced back to the individual's character. One of my Christian friends said that if God wants to punish someone that the first thing God takes away from the person is character. When we demonstrate ourselves to be good natured, and have a positive character, it becomes easy to have relationships with people from various cultures and nationalities. The connections we make should be intentional, timely, and based on value sharing.

Character

In order to stay in our lanes, we need to get along with people. It is impossible to get along with people without having a good character. This is what I decided to teach my first daughter by naming her Iwalewa (Iwalewa means "Character is beauty"). I want to ingrain this value system in her consciousness as early as possible. The real blessing of life is to have a positive spirit which makes it possible to attract good things.

When I think about character, my dad easily comes to mind. My dad had always been enterprising and good at his job, but he would not bend his rules when his bosses asked him for certain favors. People believe he could have achieved more than he achieved (a better career path) if he had bent a bit more to the whims of his employers. However, he chose to live with the integrity of his values. I cannot count the number of times my mum narrated different stories with good character as a lesson. **Your success stops where your character stops and you can never rise beyond the limitations of your character.**

The other day, as I was walking through the hallway at my university, I saw a student. I greeted her nicely, asked how her day was going, then gave her a compliment and walked away. A few minutes later, I found out she was my newly matched mentee from the mentoring program that I take part in, and that I would be mentoring her for a year. The mentor-mentee program entails meeting every week with the mentee and reporting to the school about the progress of our connection. I was happy our first conversation was great. She was respectful and she communicated with me very well. The first conversation served as the foundation for our communication during that year, in fact, our relationship thrived to the extent that she volunteered to support my PhD research endeavors. We even published a research paper together and we are still in good communication up till today.

Self-Celebration

It is great to have big dreams and work towards them. However, along the journey towards achievement of those dreams, we must learn to celebrate our milestones. Every little victory counts. During a podcast session hosted by my fellow John Maxwell Team member, he asked, "how leaders should celebrate victories". I told him that leaders should celebrate small victories because If you do not celebrate your little victories, you will become too tired to achieve your big victories. **You should celebrate being on a journey that will reveal new opportunities to you.**

Communication Skills

Writing and speaking at various levels forced me to think more about the whole essence of communication. As a public speaker, I had to be less invested in the speech itself and more invested in being understood. We cannot shout our way into being understood and if being able to raise our voice was the only requirement, many people would be public speakers today. **We must connect to communicate effectively.**

When I quarreled with my wife, it is often because I was too busy speaking that I did not hear what she was trying to say. In these cases, there was simply no communication, just shouting going on between both sides. Most of the things we hear, we need time to process so that we can act appropriately. **Communication with people should be memorable to be effective.**

Some people like to blame their poor communication on factors such as accents and intonation. However, this is unfair and misleading. Yes, there are accents. However, there is nothing like a bad accent. When I first arrived in the United States for my master's degree, I had to take trains and buses to attend the Seminar for International Teaching Assistants (SITA) on Saturdays. Whenever I missed a train or bus, it would take me the whole day to get back to my room. During the SITA training, I learned how to pronounce words better by breaking the words into syllables before pronouncing the words; I also learned how to talk slowly and speak louder than the average person because of my Nigerian accent. I found the SITA training was very helpful. However, SITA training handled only one side of the story. The other side of the story is to teach students to become better listeners. An accent only appears to be bad if the listener has poor listening skills. What if we consciously work on our listening skills? Will the world become a better place? What do you think?

Research shows that millions of dollars are lost every day by organizations simply because of poor listening skills, not bad accents (source: www.managementissues.com). Poor listening leads to upsetting other people's feelings and loss of team cohesion. As a matter of fact, poor listening skills is one of the top reasons why partners cheat in relationships. (I have never seen a reasonable person that cheated on their spouse because of a bad accent, mark my word REASONABLE). A major problem in relationships is always poor listening skills. Poor listening leads to assumptions and misunderstandings. These assumptions and misunderstandings lead to errors, ineffective decisions, and costly mistakes. Good listening requires an active, conscious choice of being conversant with your environment, state of mind, bias, exposure, and hearing condition.

I believe that most people do not really want to put much effort into listening, they are afraid; we are afraid that if we set our own perspective aside for a moment and truly strive to understand another person's point of view, one of these things may happen:

1. We will be perceived as supporting the idea, even if no agreement exists.
2. We will learn something that shows us that our own point of view is incomplete.
3. We will not get a chance to voice our opinion.

Any of these things can hinder good communication, yet we still blame it on the bad accent. Regardless of how different an accent may sound, you should be able to hear and understand what that person is saying, if you listen carefully, especially if other individuals are able to understand what is being said. Accents should not be a barrier for you, if your listening skills are good and you are truly culturally aware of your environment.

I have been guilty of poor listening too. I was at a research conference and I heard a presenter answering questions about her presentations. She sounded like a siren to my ears when she was talking. She made my ears scratchy and hurt so badly that I had to move away as fast as I could. Surprisingly, other people were enjoying her presentation and it made me realize that I must work on my listening skills.

If we persist with poor listening skills, it's only a matter of time before we destroy our relationships and alienate innocent individuals. For example, at the end of our Toastmasters meeting, a member mentioned the word "contemporary". I have reason to believe her pronunciation was right and the expression on another member's face indicated she was right. However, for some reason, a third person in the group did not understand her clearly and she had to repeat the word a couple of times. If the member is someone like me, she might hesitate before communicating during next meeting. **To prevent estrangement, we should focus on the person speaking and make mental efforts to understand them before we conclude that their pronunciation is not understandable.**

Now, I am going to tie the next few streetlights to listening, and this is because communication is so crucial to productivity. And besides, these skills are not mutually exclusive. They all complement each other.

Health Condition

How is your hearing? When was the last time you visited an audiologist? A study based on standard hearing examinations by Frank R. Lin (MD, PhD), John K. Niparko (MD), and Luigi Ferrucci (MD, PhD), concluded that one in eight individuals in the United States aged 12 years old or older, has hearing loss in both ears. Not all the individuals with bad listening habits can become a better listener without proper ear examination and treatment. It may be a good practice for organizations to perform regular ear examination for its employees to ensure excellent communication among the employees.

Environment

How quiet is your environment when you try to listen to people? I can remember an incidence when a customer care personnel described my voice as a "mumbling sound". She was frustrated by her inability to understand me, even though her fan and my fan were on and whirring in the background, naturally drowning out my voice. This caused my voice to become naturally drowned out. Excellent communicators take a moment to eliminate all the distractions in their environment before they start communicating.

State of Mind

Are you stressing about something you cannot currently do anything about? If so, why are you stressing about it? When your stress levels are elevated, **you show confusing non-verbal signals, lose control of your emotions and are likely to misunderstand what other people are communicating**.

Prejudice & Bias

Some individuals act like people who look dissimilar to them speak as if they are from another planet. These is nothing wrong with "sounding black" or "sounding country" or "sounding Hispanic." It is not right to judge people based on their accent. It is a disadvantage, and morally incorrect, to judge people solely based on their outward appearance. **We can learn a lot from listening to the experiences and perspectives of those who are different from ourselves.**

Exposure

How many cultures have you witnessed? When was the last time you traveled outside your state or country? Exposure to new cultures and different ways of thinking will allow you to understand the world better.

Gratitude

You cannot effectively show your appreciation by staying silent. Do not admire people from a long distance - take steps closer to show your gratitude. You need to act to properly appreciate a person. Better still, why not keep a gratitude journal? Do not forget small acts of kindness, saying "thank you" is a simple way of assuring your benefactor that you are coming back. Being kind should not make you feel stressed. Gratitude comes from thinking about and writing down the blessings you have received. You can count your blessings by writing them down or talking to someone about it (this is what we call testimony in the Christian faith). If you make observations about your environment, most people who are ungrateful do not think about their blessings or count them.

Oftentimes, the things you want make you forget the things you have. If you do not remember things you have, you cannot remember the things you want clearly. The solution is this- become more grateful by taking your mind off the things you want and for instance, spending more time thinking about the things you have already. We need to let people know when they are doing well, not only when they are doing badly. There is a natural scarcity of words of affirmation. Words of affirmation are not the same as unnecessary praises. In my case, I become extremely shy when someone praises me because I did not receive many words of affirmation as a child, especially from my dad. I had to work on learning how to accept compliments without feeling shy.

If you can think, you can be grateful. Things are not always as as good as they appear, and things are not always as bad as they seem. Be happy with your progress rate. The easiest way to attract the good things in people's lives is to appreciate those things in their lives. This is a natural and spiritual principle of life. It works for everyone who uses it regardless of social class or background. Pastors use this a lot in the church to raise money for the purpose of spreading the gospel. Why would you not take advantage of a natural principle like this?

Do not condition your mind to not extend your appreciation to other people due to your own struggles and suffering. In addition, do not overdo appreciation for others. Some people think appreciation is a creative way of hiding incompetence. However, balance is key. Gratitude is an attitude required to discover more about oneself. Be thankful for everything. **A grateful heart is generous to others. Do not expect someone who is not grateful to be generous to you as this is a waste of time.**

Generosity

When you become really grateful, the next thing is to give out something in your possession. Everyone has something to give. If you find it difficult to discover your own path, or maximum potential, help another person to discover their path. While you are aiding that person in discovering their own path, your path will ultimately become clearer. This basic principle of life is called the Law of Seedtime and Harvest. If you diligently plant, you will harvest one day. It is just a matter of time. The only things that should be difficult for us to give are things that we have not been given. That is, by default, nothing.

Relationships

Some people can easily tell whether you are for them or against them. However, some will need you to hurt them first before they know where they stand with you. The difference between these two groups of people is the relational intelligent quotient (RIQ). Those who have high relational IQ's have a higher chance of not being frustrated in life, a higher chance of staying in their lane and, consequently, a higher chance of success. The right and relevant people will always keep us on our track. The first relationship that is important and responsible for my success is the relationship with God. Make an intentional effort to recognize relationships that are relevant to your journey. Have a vision and surround yourself with people who believe in you. The more vulnerable you are, the more humane you are. The more humane you are, the more people can connect with you. The more people can connect with you, the higher the chance of you discovering yourself and living your full potential. The problem is that we want to look good all the time and this is not humanly possible. Sometimes we forget that however bad the situation is, we are still doing better than most people around us.

Be yourself and stop worrying about wanting everyone to like you. Everybody cannot like you. If you cut your head into pieces and gave it to someone in a bid to satisfy them, that person may still ask you why you did not cut it more slowly. During my tenure as an honorable student representative at Obafemi Awolowo University, we were allowed to make a motion to impeach an executive in the faculty of Agriculture due to misbehavior. This experience made me more aware of how to cope with people whom I disagree with, but I must work with to achieve a goal. The goal in this case was to create a safe and supportive environment for all students in the School of Agriculture, Obafemi Awolowo University, Nigeria. Having a healthy human connection with others is like having fresh air to breathe. Draw strength from the well that never runs dry - the godly and goodly people around you. I wish I could tell you that there is a formula to calculate or determine the *goodness or badness* in humans. That would save all of us the stress and waste of resources that comes with finding good relationships.

One of the popular quotes I enjoy from the acclaimed writer, Maya Angelou is this "When people show you who they are, believe them the first time." If you do not believe people the first time, they might become aggressive or suicidal when they show you the second time as people do not like to be ignored. **Do not get too busy to make real human connections: Greatness is contagious: rub minds with great people.**

Before I left Nigeria in 2014, I worked four different jobs. I worked in a restaurant as an Assistant Manager, I reared chicken, I assisted with making fried goat heads ("asun" as it is called in Yoruba), and I taught elementary level students. When I came to America, I got married and in order to support myself and my family, I had to engage in four different part-time jobs while in my PhD program.

I found this tough and almost impossible to make real connections with my family and friends. At one point, I had to stop two of my jobs so that I could have more time to pursue human connections with my family, as well as my research and writing. **There is no easy story, and sometimes on your journey, you must reappraise your progress to make time for effective relationships.**

Do not trust someone who says he has no secret: The best one can do is to ensure that the secret is not a burden to another person. Some people go to the extent of lying to keep their secrets safe. Maybe this is why my father used to say, "you may not be able to say the truth every time, but you must be seen with the truth." I did not understand this statement until I became a young adult, and I began to understand that reasonable people do not need perfection from me because perfection is overrated. **It is either we always make everything about us perfect or we prioritize connecting with people.**

Surround yourself with people who are not afraid to tell you the truth. For instance, at a point in my life I was seriously considering changing my local church, because I had grown uncomfortable with the messages I was hearing. However, I decided to wait longer to learn about what I did not want to hear before making my decision. This allowed me to expand my reasoning about what I did not like, and eventually, I fully understood why changing my church was a good idea.

When I meet a person for the first time, I usually have an urge to throw my business cards at them like excess junk food. However, my friend Ozzie Gillion taught me that it is more productive to talk to people first until the discussion leads to an exchange of business cards. Now, I wait until the discussion is leaning towards a possible future interaction before I bring out my business card for the purpose of exchange. By doing this, I am not wasting the money I used to print the business cards and I am not being overly pushy towards my new contact.

Create boundaries so people don't misuse your time but be approachable. Do not assume people will say or do the right thing during your interaction with them. People tend to do what is easy for them, not what you think they should do. Do not allow people to interfere with your mind as this reduces your effectiveness. Our minds determine our thoughts, and our thoughts determine our actions. A mindset is a fixed mental attitude that determines a person's response or interpretation of a situation. Avoid constant interaction with small-minded people like you avoid infections and plagues. Small-minded people will always give bad advice that can make you run into accidents (such as regrets and failures) on your journey through life. It is okay to talk to small-minded people, but, talking to them for too long, can shrink your mind and reasoning.

Prepare for life's difficult moments. One of these moments is receiving negative feedback. I remember when I was the President of our Toastmasters club, a guest compared my club to another club, and conclude that we were doing badly. I felt bad for some minutes, but I got over it and took actions to improve the club. Today, our club is doing a much better because I did not stay on the ground after receiving the negative feedback.

You should never get too comfortable; be the first to make a move, open yourself up and create the connection that you have been looking for. Make other people's work easy because people love people who make their lives easier. If you are a communicator, your job is to make listening easy.

Put others first, but do not forget about yourself. You are looking out for other people with yourself as the mirror. Do not take people for a ride, instead take a ride to them and they will never forget their ride with you. You cannot build an empire if you do not try to build your relationships first. As a result of understanding this reality of life, I have become a serial networker; I believe our network is our net worth. Most of my achievements have been, facilitated by the influential and supportive people I know.

Social media fosters interaction, though not as effectively as meeting in person. However, in certain instances such as the coronavirus pandemic, social media appears to be the major way to connect with people and make money. Sometimes we must be flexible with situations.

It is important to have communication etiquette and not to speak over people. I zone out when people hijack a conversation and will not give room for others to speak; it does not matter what they say, or how long they chose to talk. From what I know, this is the same for most people as well. As the saying goes, "people don't care how much you know, if they don't know how much you care". There are relationships that leave indelible marks in our lives. One of such kind of relationship in my life is with friends who have given me nicknames. One of my nicknames, Smile Virus, was given to me by one of my high school friends because during our high school days, he thought my smile was contagious.

Be supportive. However, don't be responsible for irresponsible people. You can try to buy them out with support if necessary, so that they do not show up again.

"To err is human and to forgive is divine". I believe that one of the pillars that hold relationships together is forgiveness. I have been forced to forgive myself for mistakes I have made and as well as forgive other people for their mistakes. I learned that when I forgive, I become free from emotional baggage that would otherwise make going through life more tiring and difficult. Just like it is discourteous to speak to someone without looking at them, it is discourteous to try to have a relationship with people without first knowing their names. People's names are the sweetest sound to their ears. I went to a Christmas party at the College I teach in 2019; I collected the bag of raffle tickets so that I could learn the names of the participants and connect them with the resources they needed.

Wealth is a combination of hard work + relationships + opportunities. If one of these is missing your chance of building long-lasting wealth is slim. Outline the important things and work out the details later with people in your inner circle. Just like my mum used to say: "a little here, a little there, does the magic when it comes to building relationships".

Worring lead to errors. Errors lead to more errors. More errors lead to misfortunes. Nobody wants to be with an unfortunate person. Therefore, avoid having worries at all costs. Nobody has a monopoly on knowledge, and you can learn from anyone no matter how dull you might think the person is. I learned that knowledge and wisdom are not always located in the people that you expect to find them in; sometimes knowledge and wisdom are found in the least-expected places.

Hearing the news that a dead relationship has come to life is like music to my ears. Often, we need to hold a candle up to another person for that dead relationship to come back to life. Most people become positively disposed to a relationship when they receive unexpected assistance or support from the person, they previously had a disagreement with. When a dead relationship come back to life new doors of opportunities are opened to the individuals in the relationship.

To employers reading this: Hire people to do what they know how to do best and give them the space to make mistakes so that they can learn from these mistakes.

When you invest in people, you go far. I know people who do not believe in going out of their way for other people, sometimes including their own children sometimes. You must change your ways! Family is the best thing that will ever happen to you.

Do not get mad when people offend you! Many of their actions will not matter to you in a year! Take more naps! Get over yourself, but do not get ahead of yourself. Surround yourself with people who do what you do. To do this, I started mastermind discussions on leadership and communication.

Words matter. They are the key to effective relationships. Be conscious about your choice of words. There are some words that are simple and magical, you should incorporate them into your daily diction: "I am proud of you." "Thank you." "I am sorry." "Please." "Bless you." These are some of the words and phrases that my wife and I considered necessary to teach our 3-year-old daughter. She is so used to these positive words that she now says them for fun - even when they are not necessary.

Do not wait until you need help from others before you show that you care for them. An experience that my wife had comes readily to mind. One evening, she texted her sisters-in-law to check if she was available the following day. The sister-in-law texted back, "no". When she came back, my wife was nice and asked, "How was your night? Hope you enjoyed yourself?" She was hopeful that her sister-in-law would change her mind the following day. However, her sister-in-law did not change her mind. You must touch a heart before asking for help.

Friendship is better than dating because people tend to pretend during the dating period. Unfortunately for men, women are better at pretending because they are more emotionally intelligent. To me it seems that it is a lost battle for men. My only advice to men is do not bother to fight it. To connect and not just communicate with people, you must go out of your way to make the lives of people better. You can be happy for people without expecting anything in return. If one of us wins, then all of us win.

If you want everybody to like you, then do nothing with everything you know. Knowledge and passion are powerful when they are aligned. However, people get intimidated when they see a passionate person. Usually, people need time to overcome their intimidation so they can act appropriately. There is nothing that inspires me more than a group of energetic individuals who are living intentionally based on their clear knowledge and passion.

Sometimes, the relationships we do not consider to be important turn out to be life changing. There are people in your life you are probably taking for granted right now. Sadly, this lack of appreciation may work against you in future. You need to be careful. Treat people nicely, especially your service men: mechanic, doctor, accountant etc. For instance, your annoyed mechanic can make your car brakes non-functional, leading to a fatal accident. Your offended doctor can decide to forget a surgical knife inside your body just because you did not talk nicely to him or her. Your resentful accountant can make you think you are rich while you are facing bankruptcy. Treat people with respect!

Do not be worried about getting people involved in the mess and crisis that you are experiencing in your life. Most people do not mind getting their hands dirty. Besides, most people are empathetic to challenges because they have had their fair share of troubles as well.

Ask for what you want. We assume that people know what we want, and we get upset if they do not give us those things. However, like the saying goes, "a closed mouth is a closed destiny, and a closed mouth can never be fed." To get a favor, you will need to make a request. However, you must make a connection with people before asking for help or favor. Social connections can lead to romance for people looking for love, and a business connection can lead to opportunities for people looking for money.

Wisdom is important in relationships; people make mistakes, so slow down before you write them off. Give people the benefit of the doubt regardless of any negative information you have heard about them as this will help you discern the truth. Again, I'll say this: Forgive people for their mistakes. People go through serious challenges in life: ask them about what they are going through before you conclude that they do not care about you.

Strive to make a good first impression. Most people like to test drive a car before they buy. Similarly, people like to peep into your personality before they invest all their time into having a relationship with you. Relationships are about first impressions; it takes a little time before you know who made a good one and who came short.

You can't always solve people's problems. Sometimes what people need is for you to analyze their situation, or to have an ear that will listen - not for you to solve their problem. We often spend a lot of time asking people questions about their predicament. Even though these questions are against their wishes. Hence, too much familiarity breeds contempt, if the familiarity is not appreciated.

Relationships with inanimate objects can strike an emotional chord in you. They can make you feel good and regain your confidence. I embarrassed myself at a New Year's party in 2020 by singing off-key. To partially redeem myself from that embarrassing situation, I brought out my guitar, dusted it off, and started playing. This example is why it is important to have various habits and skills. Connect with people through your experiences, this will prove valuable to you in time.

Eat one serving of food at a time as you might be embarrassed at the urge to visit the bathroom frequently if you take more than one serving. However, the new world of buffet parties has made it nearly impossible for us to abstain from excessive eating and drinking. I remember something humorous my former teacher used to say, "a big stomach is filled with big failure".

Pay attention to your community as it is important to build goodwill with the community. Do not resort to short-term personal gains as a trade-off against long-term community benefits. People you see on your way going up are the same people you will see on your way going down. Unfortunately, there will be times we go a little bit down since life is full of ups and downs, not "ups and ups."

Examine your relationship with words and speak positively. Words make a great impact on us, especially if we hear the words repeatedly. I recall advising one of my friends to stop jokingly calling my daughter "Palemo" (meaning a servant that clears the plate). I think the person meant my daughter likes tidying up and has a penchant for cleanliness, but the negative meaning is not good in the long term for a child's confidence. In my youth, my mum sewed suits for my brothers and me. I confessed that my suit would not be ready, and, to my surprise, two of my brothers' suits were ready but my suit was not (this caused me to almost miss having a nice suit). People joked that this only happened because I grew my upper teeth first as a baby; according to folk wisdom, this gives a child special powers to predict the future. I think that is not true. There is power in our confessions no matter the teeth that came out first.

There are many aspects of my life and many people I had the privilege to relate to. Some of these people are my students. I remember one incident, at the end of my climate change class, one of my students asked me to give names of three Nigerian artists, whose songs I listened to. It was a difficult pick, but I picked three artists. I was surprised and pleased that I had built rapport with my students that allowed them to feel comfortable with asking me about my choice of music. This is how it should be! Do not dismiss any aspect of your life while building relationships.

To whom much is given much is expected. This means everyone is given something that the world needs. Although some may have more to give than others, everyone still has something they can give.

A popular saying, I like is "you can be happy always or be right always". You can't achieve both at the same time. Even though I do not like too much praise, I also do not like the way I feel when I am wrong. Being wrong sometimes makes me feel like throwing up and, at other times, makes me feel like becoming a vapor. Being wrong sometimes makes me feel like I must use the bathroom. On the other hand, I have observed that people like it when I am wrong. Admitting I was wrong allowed them to feel connected with me and the connection made me happy because they were happy.

Who we associate ourselves with matters? Show me your five friends and I will tell you who you are now, and who you will likely become in five years. It is easier to drive safely in your lane if you surround yourself with the right group of people. Keep a community of like-minded people who believe that there is an ordained destination which enables them to reach their full potential.

Be conscious of your relationship with time. Time is always more valuable than money. If you lose money, you can make more money. If you lose time however, you can never get it back.

Money is not really a problem if you know what you are doing. Relationships are the problem, especially if you invest all your time in the wrong ones.

Have a sense of humor, be able to take a joke, do not take yourself too seriously. I remember a fellow contestant and Toastmaster who used to call me a "little rock and roll" guy. However, I knew he meant no disrespect, so I took it lightly. People may tease you, but it does not mean they don't respect you.

Become a master in your sphere of influence because people naturally gravitate towards people, who they believe have earned competence in a particular field. For instance, I would rather get marriage counselling from someone who was married for just a day, than from someone who has only been in casual relationships for fifty years. Based on my personal experience, people often call me to talk about leadership and communications rather than financial counselling. To become an expert, I believe people should be grounded in three "well" areas: well-read, well-educated, and well-traveled. Most times these three important "wells" are linked to one another and can make you a well-rounded person. People love to interact with well-rounded people.

Find your purpose and passions. When you go to where your purpose and passions are, your relationships come along naturally. My relationship with the head of the Department of Animal Sciences, Faculty of Agriculture, when I was President of the Department Student's Association was good. I became too comfortable around him to the extent that when I had to complete my undergraduate defense assignment, he jokingly reminded me that the meeting was not the usual head of Department and President chat. The meeting was meant to finalize my research project defense for my undergraduate studies. I can say that it was easy for me to connect with him due to the mutual respect that develops between two people who are passionate about what they do.

Who you know and the people who that person you know knows partly determines your results in life. Like the saying goes, "your network is your net worth". I got my instructor job at Broward College via a fellow Toastmaster, Dr. Nilo Marin. During one of our discussions at the end of the Broward College Toastmasters meeting, I found out that Dr. Marin was a professor at Broward College. Coincidently, the same campus where I had been trying to get a job as an adjunct instructor. He told me to see him at his office so that he could introduce me to the Associate Dean. I went to his office and the rest was history. I got the job! Based on his good relationship with the Associate Dean and the recommendation he was able to give me, I was given an opportunity to prove my credentials and teaching skills.

Pour your resources into the relationships you desire. Where your treasure is, is where your heart will be. When I was growing up, my mum used to say that it is challenging to build a child and a house at the same time. I know what she meant by this now, as I have had to make investments in caring and providing for my daughters. My family is my ultimate relationship and I channel my resources towards them.

People say you should promise your services and work out the details later. I say work out the details and then promise your services. With business relationships, integrity is everything. When integrity is lost, everything else will be lost in a matter of time. Think about it, would you pick someone who is likeable and incompetent over someone who is competent and wicked? Strive to master your work so that you do not disappoint people when you receive an opportunity to demonstrate those skills. Learn the difference between what people have and what the world needs. You should strive to connect people with the resources they need if you want to have a long-lasting relationship with them.

People like to interact and feel comfortable around someone who can keep themselves and others secure. Nobody wants a free ride from a driver with a learner's permit or from someone who perpetually gets into accidents. I have formed a habit of remembering to lock the doors in my house twice before leaving the house because safety and security are important to me.

Ask relevant questions when you meet people. Great people ask great questions, even if their bank account is currently empty.

Leadership

I knew I was on the right track the moment I realized that I did not have to strive hard to influence people. My life influences people unintentionally. Sometimes people even walk up to me to tell me how my life influenced them. This is what is referred to as natural leadership. It is almost impossible to talk about relationships without talking about leadership. Music is to musical instruments the same way leadership is to relationships. There cannot be true leadership without relationships, the same way there cannot be good music without musical instruments. Leadership is telling full-grown men to do something they were predisposed to resist. Leadership is essentially influence for a purpose, despite the numerous definitions of leadership. Think about leadership as the ability to provide direction to a group of people you share a vision with—the aim of sharing this vision is to reach an anticipated destination together. A pack of inspired people can go further than one inspired person. Inspiring for a purpose is the basis of leadership. If you are a leader, and you achieve the same results with your team that you would have achieved on your own, then you are not leading rather you are taking a stroll by yourself. I learned this when I was the president of the National Animal Science Students

Association (NASSA). As the president, I did not give all my executives enough time to discuss and think about the group's next move. Some were able to follow easily, however, some needed more time to decide. I assumed those who needed more time did not have anything to contribute or did not want to contribute. This assumption was wrong. They had something to contribute; they were just taking their time. Whenever I decided to move on with the half of the group that made quick decisions, I would reach a roadblock when it was time to vote on the decision. My executives who did not have enough time to speak up would vote NO. Thankfully, I learned from this experience and changed my strategy. My new strategy saved me a lot of time and energy as it was to wait for the other half to decide. Inclusion is a crucial aspect of leadership. If you must wait a little longer to include all the stakeholders in a decision, please do. Also, I have learned that people align their money, time, heart, mouth, and energy in the same direction. If you give people a say in something including actions, they will be willing to put their heart, money, energy, and time in the task.

Leadership is also about discerning good advice from the followers. Human nature is the most important thing to understand as a leader. A leader is the hands and legs of followers. In other words, a leader steers the collective thoughts of a group of people because things can easily get chaotic if everyone carried out their own actions out individually. A leader reflects the thoughts and actions of the followers. A leader inspires others, and you should move with the people who inspire you. Even though my friend and fellow Toastmaster, Adi Devendra is much younger than me, he offered to be my coach for my 3 Minute Thesis presentation. I accepted because the ability to lead does not correlate with age.

A leader goes to where there is no path and leaves a trail. Self-leadership is going to that path and clearing the bush by yourself. When other people see the path that you have cleared for yourself, they will follow. The problem today is that we want people to follow a course of action or a path without showing any evidence of self-leadership. Self-leadership also requires us to educate ourselves on the formal and informal principles of leadership (compassion, empathy, dependability, integrity, loyalty, trust, vision, objectivity, patience).

Having a clear vision is another essential part of leadership. The vision needs to be clearly written out because people become what you show them repeatedly. Leaders are dangerous when they do not value human life more than they value their own personal interests and ambitions.

Most great leaders are liked by their followers. During my time at Florida Atlantic University, I had great relationship with a lot of students and staffs because I can easily connect with people and guide them to the resources that they need.

Leadership provides solutions to problems in a timely manner. Timing is very important in leadership efforts as leadership must be available at the time needed. The time to lead is as important as leading.

One single tree cannot be called a forest, the same way, a leader cannot be the alpha and omega of a leadership system. A group of people are responsible for the leadership system in a country, school, hospital, etc., not just one person.

Attitude

Attitude is everything. Our attitude towards life and people has a great effect on how we attain our maximum potential. Unfortunately, an attitude is not like a physically broken chair that we can fix with tools. An attitude can only be repaired with internal surgery and utilizing positive words. In order words, if you are not feeling positive, you can start feeling positive and do positive things again by confessing positive words. Most of the time we want to feel good and see positive results before we have a positive attitude. However, life works on the contrary - we must have a positive attitude before we can attract the positive things that we want.

On a lighter note, I read somewhere once that there are people who think that heat makes people have bad attitudes. What do you think?

Anyway, back to attitudes; I have been able to move past keeping grudges. I issue a blank check for forgiveness ahead of time to maintain my sanity. The truth is difficult times will come. Life is not about waiting for the storm to pass; it is about learning how to ride through the storm. The more positive we think, the better our attitude and the higher our chance of riding out of the storm.

Finally, having an open mind about situations is a good attitude to embrace. We should be open-minded to possible events in our lives because the mind is like a parachute – the mind only function when it is opened.

Service

Have you ever liked someone and wished that you did not like them? This is the way I feel about service. Nobody becomes truly great without service, yet service takes more from us than what we bargained for.

At the end of my college experience, this was true for me - service really was more than I bargained for. As you will agree, college is expensive. However, you don't have to pay for college all by yourself. Paying for college all by yourself means you are going to start your life with the burden of student loans. For instance, my wife had student loans to pay off immediately after we got married. This was not a great experience because we had to budget paying off her student loans into our monthly expenses. Then, while we were amidst paying off her student loans, a car loan also suddenly appeared. Anyway, that was a small digression. Service and excellent academic performances opened the door of scholarships and fellowships that protected me from the burden of student loans. During my days at Florida Atlantic University days, I was often the first in line to volunteer for projects and activities. Sometimes this meant I had to be vulnerable and risk people laughing at me. However, being vulnerable ultimately provided me with opportunities that enabled me to finish graduate school without any student loans. In addition to being loan free, I was awarded the McKnight Dissertation Fellowship from the Florida Education Fund and Graduate Fellowship for Academic Excellence from the Graduate College at Florida Atlantic University. Apart from these financial gains, collegiate and community service allowed me to discover myself while interacting with people.

Collegiate Service: I participated in Graduate Student panels during my school's orientation for incoming graduate students, and, transfer student orientation. I volunteered to be a judge at the 9th Annual Broward Student Research Symposium hosted by Florida Atlantic University. I was a Co-advisers for two honors projects. I also served as a peer mentor on different platforms. I mentored undergraduate students in their research endeavors throughout the year. I was able to motivate the students in the areas of their research interests and expand research engagement through mentoring, hosting workshops, and giving classroom presentations. I exceeded specific performance operations in conjunction with the Council of Scholarship and Inquiry. I provided creative ideas for designing new training programs for research workshops. Despite the challenges that I had during mentoring; my students have won various awards at different competitions. I am also a founding member of the "Keep Moving" club at Florida Atlantic University; This club aims to support students throughout the Covid-19 pandemic.

Community Service: I have volunteered as a judge for the 2020 National Conference on Undergraduate Research at the Montana State University. I have presented twice at the "Broward College Professional Development Day." I have volunteered for different roles during Toastmaster events including: Tie-breaker judge, Contest Master, and Timer. I have also held various leadership positions at Toastmasters: President, Vice President Education, and Sergeant at Arms. I have participated as a volunteer for multiple "Martin Luther King Jr. Day of Service" events.

I have volunteered with "The Yes Program" organized by AIESEC, Ghana. A few years ago, I was a keynote speaker at Margate Middle School. My friends at FAU jokingly described me as the guy who is everywhere volunteering and serving.

During all these engagements, I have learned the following lessons:

1. Service is leadership in training; it encourages people to respect their leaders.
2. Most of the leaders we admire today have an attitude of service.
3. Money cannot give you the fulfillment that you feel when you serve people.
4. Service says a lot about who you are and what you care about.
5. Service opens the door of uncommon opportunities and valuable relationships.

Improvement

You must engage in continuous improvement to stay on track and in your lane. You must be better today than you were yesterday. The key is constant improvement, not competition. Some people consider me competitive because of my consistent effort to improve myself. They think I am competing with them because they do not understand how life works. The biggest room we all have, is the room for improvement. Everyone can improve. My goal in life is to do better than my father and mother.

Adaptability

Spontaneous people don't like to plan, and meticulous people don't like to go with the flow. However, the middle point between the two is adaptability. My wife can be considered as the more spontaneous person in our relationship, while I am more of the planner. Many of the times, we meet in the middle ground. To make the dynamic of marriage even better, I have been working to become more spontaneous.

Life offers us minimal stability but numerous of opportunities to adapt. During my 35th birthday celebration, my Master of Ceremony had to leave the event with very short notice. Immediately, I recalled that the Master of Ceremony for my wedding was also at my birthday celebration. I asked her if she would like to continue as the Master of Ceremony for my birthday and, thankfully, she said yes. I am glad she was spontaneous in that situation.

I learned about adaptability from my mum in a hard way. Back in my youth, we would visit my mum's friends and they often offered me food to eat. My mum would usually find every possible way to communicate her disapproval to me without using words. If you are somebody like me and enjoys food, then you know visiting people and turning down their meals is not fun. In these instances, I was forced to adapt to avoid serious consequences.

You can observe adaptivity in your environment by answering the following questions:

1. Does the hot shower get colder if you stay long enough under the spray of the hot water?
2. Does the cold water in the swimming pool get warmer if you stay longer in the cold water?
3. After applying cologne or perfume, when you no longer smell the scent, can everyone around you still smell it?
4. Why do we no longer feel our clothes touching our skin shortly after putting them on?

Many successful people understand the importance of adaptability. The fact of life is things are never exactly the way we imagined them to be. Often success comes from the ability to navigate the unexpected bends and detours of life and bounce back from them. After all, even billionaires have their down times.

As a Nigerian immigrant, I had to learn adaptability in order to acclimatize to the American culture. If I did not adapt, perhaps I would not have had a shot at pursuing my own version of the American dream. We must always remember that life responds to the law of adaptability and not the law of stability.

Exercise and Hygiene

By now you might have noticed I always give examples of my mother; this is because she is one of the wisest people that I know. One of her nuggets of wisdom which I am fond of is: "if you save money at the expense of eating good food, you will spend at least twice the money in the hospital to return to normal health." This statement is most impactful when you realize that you may not be lucky enough to return to normal health. Do not compromise your health for financial gain. You cannot achieve your potential without physical capacity. Therefore, you should prioritize eating healthy and exercise. Something as simple as spending 30 - 45 minutes running or walking everyday can bring long term benefits to your body. Do not use a lack of time or lack of money to register at a gym as an excuse; If you consciously stay active, you do not have to register at a gym.

Salesmanship

Believe it or not, everybody sells something, including you. You are constantly selling yourself directly or indirectly. It is, therefore, your responsibility to brand and project yourself as having something people consider valuable. In the new age of social media, companies will pay almost any amount of money to ask celebrities, who have many followers to market their brands. Similarly, think of yourself as one of those brands on social media. How do you want people to connect with you? What values or opportunities do you want people to associate with you? Once you understand and know your value, you should go ahead and project it. Do not undersell yourself.

Showmanship

Showmanship is about aligning yourself with the law of relevance. The law of relevance states that, to be relevant, you must move with the trends. Despite the level of success, you can achieve without showmanship, showmanship can allow your influence to burn like a wildfire even while you are sleeping or inactive. It is advantageous to move with trends because a lot of people are on the same journey to see what you are doing.

However, distinguishing oneself from the crowd can become a problem along the way. Showmanship solves this problem for you by separating you from the crowd. Sometimes, to separate yourself from people on the same journey, you must be a little bit more dramatic, louder, or emotional than the rest.

Self-Belief

Self-belief is the act of deliberately having confidence in yourself and in your abilities. You cannot outsource confidence. Oftentimes, people will not believe in us unless we first believe in ourselves. If you constantly put yourself down, your close friends and family may think that you are not going to do well in life. Personally, many of my friends thought I could not go as far as having a Ph.D., but they were forced to change their opinions of me as my life unfolded. Imagine what my life would have look like if I had waited for them to believe in me before pursuing my dreams, I would have simply not reached the level of achievement that I have thus far.

Culture

Like I stated earlier, I am a Nigerian-born immigrant. I first arrived in the United States on the 14th of January in 2014. Upon my arrival I had already missed some of the classes for my master's program. To catch up with what I had missed, I promptly needed to approach one of my course mates. I walked up to one of the girls in my class and, with a heavy Nigerian accent, I said, "Hello Tatiana." She replied immediately, with her high pitch American accent said, "I have a boyfriend."

I found out later that Tatiana was not frustrated with me because I accosted her against her wish, but rather she was frustrated because I was not confident enough like a typical American when I approached her. That day, I learned a major lesson about American culture. If you are in America you must talk as if you know what you are saying, even if you do not know what you are saying. This experience made me realize that my transition into American culture was going to be rough.

Studying in America was a lot easier because when I had to study for exams in Nigeria, I sometimes used candlelight when the electricity was out. Imagine my culture shock when I started to adjust to a life with constant electricity. After my wedding, my wife suggested that we go for a candlelight dinner; Something in America had convinced her that a dinner without electricity was the epitome of romance. This "romantic" experience was traumatic for me because I had lived 30 years of my life in the dark, using candlelight to study for quizzes and exams. I performed some of my house chores in the night using candlelight as the only source of light in extreme situations.

On the flip side, when I first arrived in America, I was quite physically fit from being active and eating healthy. However, after a few weeks in America I started to get out of shape. My American friends indirectly told me I had become fat, by saying I have adjusted well to United States. I blame this on the many automatic machines in America that replace much of the physical work.

Other times, I go to social events with friends just to experience the American culture. I felt privileged to be able to observe the difference between the ways Nigerians and Americans greet each other. In Nigeria, males from a certain tribe greet the elderly by prostrating, or bowing their heads a little, and women slightly kneel. This is done because the tribe places great respect on its older population. Imagine my shock when I realized that in the United States, you can lean in and peck an elderly person as a form of greeting.

It is to your overall advantage to take the time to understand and appreciate other cultures. The world is continually leaning towards diversity. The more you know about cultures different from your own, the more valuable you are perceived in the workplace and various other settings. This is one of the reasons a lot of job seekers are completing the diversity and inclusion certification now. This shift in value system is one of the things that has motivated me to learn Spanish, French, and Creole.

We named our second daughter Mojuolalo. Mojuolalo is a Yoruba-Nigerian name which means "I am better than wealth." At the time she was conceived, my family had some pressing financial constraints, however when she was born, she opened the door to financial abundance. In the Nigerian (Yoruba) culture, we tend to give names based on the circumstances of the birth or our prayers for the future, whereas that is not quite the case here in the United States.

All of this is to say that you must acclimatize to the environment you find yourself, even if it is not a new country. There is always something to change or relearn in order to achieve your potential.

Responsibility

Being responsible often involves your commitment to a situation or path that you choose. It is deciding that you are in the game for the long haul and you will do what is required to make things work. A good example here is family; you commit to loving and caring for your family members, even during difficult and problematic times. You also commit to provide for those you are directly responsible for, such as your spouse, kids, and other members of the family.

Sacrifice

A major milestone achievement in my life as a chess player is when I developed the skills to sacrifice a highly valuable chess piece (for example, the queen) for a less valuable chess piece (for example a pawn) on the chess board to create a win or checkmate. Generally, most of us can give away a big thing if we know a bigger thing is on the way. But how many people can sacrifice without expecting anything in return or without knowing what they will receive in return?

Our sacrifice to humanity, or God (depending on what you believe), can be so powerful that it will someday be talked about all over the world. These sacrifices might bring us great relationships, that we never imagined we could have. If we believe in sacrificial living through giving, we can connect with great minds. All chess blitz players understand that time is a major factor for winning in a 5-minute chess game. Make your next move your best move!

Rest

It is important to take a break from time to time. If you can afford to, go on a vacation. We cannot effectively think or function if our daily schedule is too busy. I prefer to take naps or go to sleep when my body is demanding rest from me. Even while I am working, I make it a priority to take 1-2 minutes break for every 45 minutes. Resting give us the ability to produce the best in an excellent state of mind. Resting also lowers the chance of having unnecessary fight in the workplace.

Emotion

If you learn to play to people's emotions, you will achieve a lot. Have you ever wondered why you are intrigued by the trailer of a movie? This is because the producers have learned to play into your feelings by showing you emotional or suspenseful highlights of the film. In business relationships, you can become successful through understanding, and using, human emotions. Think: How can I generate excitement? How can I generate love? How can I generate ambition? The world is controlled by emotions such as love, hate, sympathy, and empathy. Expressing emotions leads to more meaningful human connections and ultimately aid you in your path to success.

Entertainment

Boredom can drive people away from you because people like to be entertained and enjoy themselves. People's hearts are stollen through humor and laughter. In a world of routine, entertainment is the lifeline for happiness and joy.

Education

In Nigeria, many families believe that a solid education is the best legacy you can give to children. We value academic excellence in Nigeria so much so, that even without electricity, we read by candlelight just to pass our exams. Education for many middle-class families opens the door for opportunities to have a more affluent life. Good education can further empower people to challenge the status quo and improve their environment. While I do not necessarily believe a formal education is the only pathway to success, I do believe that successful people have a deliberate commitment to continually learn and become more educated.

Avoid Scamming

A few years ago, I told my wife that my sister would be coming from Nigeria to stay with us as she attended graduate school. My wife later told me that she was not sure that my sister was really my sister; My wife believed that she could very well be a wife that I had kept in Nigeria. To allay her fears, I showed her my sister's birth certificate. She was still doubtful because of the stories she had heard about Nigerians. That was when the perception of Nigerians, including myself, really dawned on me. Although disheartening, I was able to understand the source of her fear; Many Nigerian men have been known to deceive unsuspecting women overseas while they lead a double life. These scams have a negative rippling effect - they may provide a way of escape for one man, but they cause trouble for another. It is important that your lifestyle does not create a stereotype that implicates other people's lives. It is also important that while you are on your journey to actualizing your potential that you avoid lumping groups of people together, or assuming everybody is the same. You must strive to know people on their own merit and give everyone the benefit of doubt.

Finally, regardless of the assumptions people make about you, remember that you have the power to be whatever you want to be. Inside you there is something that can never be found inside any other person. You need to discover that *"thing"* on the inside that distinguishes you from another person. You need to find your punch line and deliver it. Strive to make a difference in all that you do. It is not about what others are doing or not doing, it is about what you do with opportunities that you have. It is easy to assume all Nigerians or

Americans are scammers. However, in doing so, you will miss out on some incredible opportunities these people can provide.

Values

Deliberately gravitate towards people who have similar values as you. If someone shares the same values with you, it is more likely that both of you will be happy with the interaction. To accomplish this, you must know your value first!

One of my dearest values is humility. Humility does not mean wearing dirty clothes or allowing people to step on you; Humility is allowing others to shine by helping them, even when you do not think they deserve your support. Humility is not discouraging people from recognizing your hard work, rather it is being able to laugh at yourself before people can laugh at you.

On the other hand, pride often makes people believe that they can behave badly towards others. Yet, when the same people who they are treating badly, treat them badly, they are not allowed to do so. You are not prideful if you can help someone who you are not happy with and can allow another person to outshine you in some respects.

People

Value people and your relationship with them. A remarkable thing about people is that if you help them get what they want, they will help you get what you want. There are unseen forces that obligate them to help you, even if they do not want to. That is why many organizations use the catch phrase, "People first." Most of the things you hope to achieve cannot be achieved without the help of others. I try to treat people better than I want to be treated. Despite how hard it can be to treat mean people nice, doing so brings us the positive results that we all desire. People do not always remember what we say, but they will always remember how we make them feel.

On your journey to reaching your full potential, you can apply these three key points to your life:

1. Know your values.
2. Teach people your values and the way you want them to treat you.
3. Treat people better than you expect them to treat you.

Sexual Purity

As a child born into a Christian family, at a very young age the idea of sexual purity was indoctrinated in me – this value guided me through my adult relationships. The truth is, committing to sexual purity and having integrity in your romantic relationships will often get tested, even when you are married. I remember a trip I took recently to a research conference. For this conference I booked a hotel and, late in the night, I heard a knock on my door. I decided to check it out because my first thought was that it was an emergency. I walked towards the back door and shifted the blind to the side. To my surprise I saw an old white lady panicking as if she needed help.

She said, "I know you are from Nigeria, and you just checked in tonight, do you want this?"

At this point, I had a lot of questions going on in my head. Who was she? How did she know my name? How did she know my country of origin?

I tried to convince myself that I did not hear her properly and thought she meant something entirely different. I genuinely thought someone was pulling a prank on me and that I would wake up in the morning to see a viral picture or video of me on YouTube, or some other social media platform. I waited for her to say she was joking but she did not; This old woman was truly trying to offer me sex. She proceeded to lift her skirt up and show me her underwear.

At this point I had two options: Say "yes" and sleep with this woman who was right in front of me or say "no" and control my instincts. This was a perfect opportunity to answer a question fueled by sexual pleasure: What is the difference between having a sexual experience with a white woman and a black woman? I also wondered why this lady was interested in a poor black man like me when she could be interested in the various old, rich, white men that America has to offer. Had someone told her Nigerien men are sexually proficient? Then, I remembered statistics that I once read - according to a report by the Nigerian Voice, an increasing number of African men are in long-term relationships with white women.

Further, according to the Pew Research Center, black men are twice as likely as black women to have a spouse who is a different race or ethnicity (24 percent vs. 12 percent). Perhaps the white lady at my door was trying to be part of these statistics which show that an increasing number of black men are no longer as interested in black women. Maybe this woman thought she could test run these statistics by being with me. My reasoning permeated the situation and I remembered that real men do not buy girls. I closed the door and went back to my bed. Five seconds after I laid back in bed, my phone rang. It was my wife! I was in shock by the short interval of time between the incident with the old white woman and my wife's call. I picked up the phone with my voice still a little shaky.

When I picked up the phone my wife said, "Hello Love, how are you doing?" "The Lord told me you are a good man."

That was her only reason for calling me. I now see why some men are too quick to call women witches; Women are heavily intuitive, and this frustrates men a lot. I wonder what the lord would have told my wife if I took up the old woman's offer. Do you know? Maybe the Lord would have told her, "Hold on, he is busy." "Give him a few minutes to complete what he started." Jokes aside, even to this day I have not asked my wife if she sent a prostitute to my hotel room, or if she knows about the encounter. If you were in that situation, what would you have done? Sexual integrity is important because, throughout your life, you will find yourself in circumstances that you had not anticipated.

Time

One of the best things you can gift yourself is learning how to manage your time. What you can do today, do today and do not wait until tomorrow. Procrastination kills destiny; Procrastination kills faster than any deadly disease known to man. If you are supposed to do something, and you can do it, accomplish it right away. If you cannot do it right away, write it down and create a plan to do it later. I am still haunted by my lost opportunity for a college award nomination simply because I forgot to submit the application on time. Procrastination often can cost you an open door.

Memorability

Memorability is the quality or state of being easy to remember, and more importantly, worth remembering. To be memorable you must leave a bit of yourself everywhere you go. I do not mean that you should forget your phone or wallet when you are visiting your friends, but rather, leave a bit of yourself through having meaningful conversations and taking actions that are in line with what you believe. By doing so, even if people forget your name, they will not forget the impactful things you said or did. When we first meet people, we only have approximately two minutes to have a memorable conversation about something we care about. Due to this, it is always good to be prepared. I recommend having an elevator pitch speech prepared to give to the people you hope to meet; This will make you appear more knowledgeable and confident. For example, if you had the opportunity to meet the former President, Barack Obama, and speak to him for 2-minutes, what would you say in those 2-minutes?

Innovation

Innovation entails finding new ways of thinking or doing things. Sometimes we must think of a new idea quickly on our journey to fulfill our maximum potential. I exercise my innovative powers as a speaker. I am a Toastmaster with the distinguished education levels of Advanced Communicator Bronze (ACB) and Advanced Leader Bronze (ALB). I had to deliver numerous speeches and engage in various leadership projects to attain these educational levels. As a member of Toastmasters, I am expected to deliver speeches from a manual of my choice. After completing the basic manual in the traditional pathways that Toastmasters offers, I was able to pick a manual from the advanced communication series; From this, I picked the entertaining speaker. In the entertaining speaker series, there were five projects for me to complete. One of these projects was to give a speech on a personal experience with the intent of entertaining the audience. I decided that I would talk about something uncomfortable in a comfortable and funny way; The title of my speech was "What Is Your Farting Angle?". In the speech I spoke about constructing chairs with a flatulence angle that is specific to an individual's body structure. Farting angle is, therefore, the angle between the buttocks and the surface of the chair which allows for the lowest sound and minimal odor.

I came up with this story to demonstrate my on-the-spot innovative thinking skills. The lesson that I tried to sell was this: What if we could reduce the sound and odor from farts by constructing chairs that successfully muffle the fart? This idea could save us a lot of embarrassment on dates. Everybody has a million-dollar idea or a million-dollar gift. The question is, are you going to act on it or not? For example, I hate throwing things away and I have a passion for recycling. Most people I know just throw things away without thinking twice or cringing - that is not in my DNA. Ideas for innovation is given in puzzle pieces; You must write them down or type them out to have a complete piece when it is time to act.

Feedback

There is a common saying that goes "receiving feedback is an act of love." This adage comes from the idea that when we receive feedback, it helps us to improve. However, feedback, especially when it is critical, can be hard to receive. I remember one of my professors jokingly telling me that I was proud. I could have easily ignored this comment, except, one of my siblings had also suggested that my body language reeked of pride. When my sibling gave me this critique, I tried to explain that I had waited for this moment my whole life; I used to be the shy, ugly, and awkward looking kid. I found my voice and my purpose as I grew out of this undesirable phase, so I wanted people to know about it. It was never my intention to exhibit a prideful energy because I believed that I was just being myself. The truth is, you cannot stay in your shell solely because you do not want to give people the wrong impression. At the same time, you also need to listen to what other people have to say as it might give you a window to appraise yourself and become better.

Reflection

Although feedback is great, you have a responsibility to reflect on the information that you receive. Reflection occurs when you take the time to think about your actions, thoughts, and the feedback you have received. It is easier to be honest with yourself when you are alone and left to ponder about your life. The only requirement of reflection is that you must be willing to keep an open mind and admit to yourself the areas that need to be improved.

Reading

After you have reflected on the steps you have taken, it is beneficial to create time to read works of various authors in the fields that you are interested in. I create time to read books on my areas of interests. I read books on science, research, writing, speaking, leadership, music, and humor. These books guide my future journey because I learn from the mistakes, failures, and success of the authors. Reading has also developed my critical thinking skills and problem-solving skills. My friends ask about my solution to certain challenges and sometimes the solution comes to my mind as if it was saved in my mind already.

Writing

If you read enough about a specific area of influence, then based on your understanding of this area, you will feel the need to write. Writing will give you the opportunity to examine your progress towards achieving your maximum potential. Writing has helped me to express myself in a way that opens the door for more self-awareness. Writing compelled me to think about myself and evaluate my experiences. Writing also made me understand that knowledge is progressive and not static.

CHAPTER 9

The Fast Lane of Excellence

At this point in the book, you should have a clear understanding of what it means to find your destined lane. You should also understand the values that are necessary to progress on your journey. Perhaps you are still wondering, "How can I keep things moving?" The answer is simple: Excellence. Excellence will get you to your destination much faster than playing it safe or being an average joe.

Unfortunately, even though many of us pray to be given an excellent spirit, some of us are not ready to put in the hard work to achieve it. The book of Ecclesiastes chapter 9 verse 10 from the Holy Bible states, "Whatever your hands find to do, do it with all thy strength." Excellence projects as different roles for different people - as a boss, excellence might be as simple as genuinely caring for your employees or seeking out ways to aid their professional development. As an employee, excellence might entail staying a few extra minutes at work.

As expected, many people hate this lane because it requires them to do what they do not have to do. For me, completing my PhD, getting married, becoming a U.S. citizen, volunteering to serve, performing excellently academically, mentoring students, allowing myself to be mentored, joining the John Maxwell Team, joining

Toastmasters International, applying for fellowships, and writing this book are all intentional efforts to keep me on the fast track of my lane. None of these feats have been easy, and they have all required me to demonstrate excellence.

CHAPTER 10

Summary

The self-discovery journey is the best journey that we can engage in. As I was watching the music show, *The Voice*, the other day, I came upon a stammerer who sang so beautifully. When singing his vocal cords were seamless despite his speech being stuttered. It made me wonder: What if there is a section of our brain that is exceptionally developed and all we need to do is discover which part it is to flow in our genius? Incredible, right?

This book, although inexhaustive, was designed to help you connect with insights and daily nuggets of wisdom that can propel you towards your personal genius. Staying in your lane is necessary to reach your destination and full potential. Below are some extra nuggets that will help give you clarity and perspective as you move towards your purpose:

1. When facing challenges down the road in your area of influence, this book, *Stay in your lane,* will equip you with the necessary knowledge for winning. If you use this knowledge very well, you will be able to stay in your lane and change the world with the light that you shine.

2. Avoid maximum potential tailgating. Do not journey behind a person bigger than you in such a way that they are blocking your view of your own journey. Position yourself properly for the greatest impact.

3. To better your clarity on the journey ahead, make sure you use all of the 38 metaphorical streetlights listed in this book.

4. Create enough breathing space for yourself - devoid of distractions in your environment. Having personal space should help you reflect daily on the steps you have taken thus far.

Remember: you cannot control the winds; you can only control the sails to reach your destination. Ideas are like flashlights – to pick up the signals, you must be sensitive and quiet with your inner self. Always have writing materials with you wherever you go - remembering new ideas can help you reinvent yourself. Ignorant people believe that what will be, will always be, regardless of the effort, or lack of effort, we make to help them. What will be will be, is not true if we play a part in the process; People who do not understand this are gradually moving towards the side of fear, and not faith.

Faith is the only language that the universe can understand. Fear is counterproductive in your journey to self-actualization - you must confront your fears. Like I have stated before, fear is the greatest time waster. You must break your fears before your fears break you. Dare to be adventurous and engage in new activities. This will keep laughter in your life and turn away fears. Do not be afraid to look stupid, try new things with faith. By trying new things, you will learn something new about yourself regardless of the outcome. This new knowledge will help you throughout your journey. Besides, if you do not do stupid things when you are young, you will never have anything to smile about when you are older; Success is merely too boring to cause the kind of laughter you need in old age.

Life is an ongoing journey. I am not yet at my best yet and neither are you. The first step to achieve more is knowing that there is more. There will always be more fulfilment for those who want more. You must believe there is more, desire more, and then go for more. Growing up my mum would always hide the remaining rice in the pot from me. When I asked for more rice, she would ask me if I was asking because I was hungry, or if I was asking just because I wanted to overeat and knew that there is more rice in the pot.

You have raw talents that you need to extract and refine. Spend quality time discovering these natural talents as this is one of the best decisions you will ever make. Do not be discouraged by little setbacks you may have now - stay in your lane no matter what. I have heard people say passion and gifts do not put food on your table. This might be true in some cases, but passion and gifts can put things that are better than food on your table; Passion will put fulfillment, rest, peace of mind, and generational wealth on your table.

CHAPTER II

Conclusion

If you had the opportunity to start your life all over, what would you do differently? What activities, skills, or passions would you pursue? I remember in the beginning of 2020 I was asked what my new year's resolution would be. I decided that even if it meant making more mistakes, my resolution would be to become more spontaneous. Life is happening fast, and I want to ensure that I am exploring all my giftings. I must keep discovering myself as well as the talents and gifts that I have. You should do the same.

The truth is, your life is a gift from God (or your own personal belief), and what you do with your life is your gift to God. You cannot go through life without knowing your gifts and passions. Knowing and engaging in what you are good at will allow you to live to your maximum capacity in life. Maximizing your potential is not about being the richest person or being happy every time - it is more about living a life that positively impacts others. Do not merely aim to make money as money is a visitor that can leave your house without informing you. You will be happy and have riches that last a lifetime if you take actions to live to your full potential and help people to do the same.

Fear prevents most people from maximizing their potential. It is also very difficult to see fear without its close cousin, jealousy. Fear and jealousy come from the same line of thought. Most people become jealous when they compare their abilities to the abilities of others. Such people eventually get angry because they cannot do the same thing that another person is doing. You should avoid fear and jealousy as much as you can. If you want to be successful, then you must resist feeling negative emotions towards the success of others. Instead of feeling badly, you should celebrate the success of other people and work hard for your own.

When you invest in discovering your gifts, you will realize that you have no business being jealous. In fact, the most ignorant thing you can do is to think someone else is better than you. If you do this then you will live in perpetual envy of that said person. I am not better than you, and the successful people you know are not better than you either. Successful people have only discovered something about themselves that you have not yet discovered. Instead of spending time being jealous and angry towards the successful people around you, use that time and energy to explore a part of yourself that has been hidden.

You need to be open-minded to walk through the doors of self-discovery. We become what we think about because our actions and life are reflections of what we spend our time thinking about. Align your thinking with the type of life you desire.

I think we all can agree that it is hard to be energetic all the time. It is even harder to control a flowing energy in a positive direction. Your job is to discover the things you can do naturally that will allow energy to flow in a positive direction; These are the activities that feel most natural to you, and to which you give your most energy. Surprisingly, these natural inclinations might indicate your passion.

The world we live in is not effort oriented, it is result-driven. Due to this, when we see people genuinely putting effort towards a particular endeavor, we think that they are not working hard enough if they cannot produce good results. The flip side of this is people appearing to do nothing yet getting results at the end of the day. When this happens, most people are eager to say that life is unfair.

Life is like a comedy concert. When a comedian speaks, and you do not get the punch line, you need to move on to the next punchline to avoid missing both; If you over think what you missed, you will also miss the next thing. Do not waste your time trying to solve past issues because time is the most precious commodity we have. Once time has passed, it cannot be retrieved. People say they are looking for closure when they do not know what to do with their time. The closure is in the experiences that you have already had.

Can you think of any celebrity who is known for excellently pursuing two or three passions at the same time? If you try, you will find that there are almost none. After reflecting on this, I resigned from two of my jobs. If resignation is going to give you the opportunity to focus on your strengths and live your full potential, then I recommend that you also resign.

We cannot choose who we are, or why we are here, but we can choose what we do. The problem with this is that it is almost impossible to get it right with the WHAT, if we do not know the

WHO or WHY. When you know your WHY, you have more options with what you can do. When you understand your WHY, your WHAT has even more impact.

Whenever I felt like giving up, I would tell myself that quitting is not an option. In every crisis, there is an opportunity. Keep going because you got this. Do not ever give up. Throughout your life there will be many times that you must reset, readjust, restart, and refocus - just do not quit. Reach for your dreams no matter who tries to talk you out of them. Dream bigger and faster than the discouragement you face. Always believe in yourself! Failure is fantastic if we learn from it. Dust up your shame and move on because life is too short. Know what you want and fight for it - fight for your happiness! Failures are only lessons learned and not setbacks. Quit being afraid to succeed! Enjoy your failures and successes. Make the mistakes and go through the hardships. Embrace the bad times as they will lead you to where you need to be.

Never stop learning and growing into who you are destined to be. How would the world be different if you were never born? Give somebody else the chance of having a better life by staying in your lane. Please remember that the world will be shortchanged if you decide to live a life that is less than what you are capable of living.

CHAPTER 12

Discovery Workbook

Activity 1

Who are you? What are the experiences that have defined who you are?

_____

_____

_____

_____

_____

_____

Activity 2

Identify one aspect of your life that you desire to become better at. Identify ten people you think are knowledgeable in this area. Now eliminate five people from the list. It will be easier for you to focus and learn from five people than it will be to learn from ten people. Below are a few qualities to look for in your top five people who will inspire your development.

Empathy

Originality

Passion to help others

Good listener

Possession of a practical footprint

Devoid of jealousy

Similar points of interest

Capacity to mentor you

Now, list the 5 people you have chosen below. You should have a one-on- one discussion with everyone on this list, one after the other.

_____

_____

_____

_____

_____

_____

Activity 3

What will you do if following your dreams requires you to move to a new location with an environmental condition that you have always avoided? How will you adapt?

_____

_____

_____

_____

_____

_____

Activity 4

Practice networking. Begin by reaching out to your neighbors and people within any of the organizations that you belong. Strike up a conversation with them, be pleasant, exchange business cards when necessary. Now think about what you learned about yourself from this experience. Write these lessons below.

_____

_____

_____

_____

_____

_____

Activity 5

Write down the name of one successful person in your area of interest that is world renowned. Once you are done, do some research about the person. Find out what he/she did to stay in his/her lane. Write the valuable aspects of their life journey down below.

_____

_____

_____

_____

_____

_____

CHAPTER 13

Reflections

1. Take a few minutes to reflect on the exercises you did in the worksheet above. How did these activities impact your self-awareness? Write your answers below.

_____

_____

_____

_____

_____

_____

_____

2. If you had unlimited resources and support, how would you spend the rest of your life?

_____

_____

_____

_____

_____

_____

_____

3. Imagine having a conversation about staying in your lane. How would you convince your listener or friend that you have discovered your lane?

_____

_____

_____

_____

_____

_____

_____

4. What advice or insights would you offer a friend who seeks to discover his/her lane?

_____

_____

_____

_____

_____

_____

_____

5. What are you willing to change about yourself that will help you stay in your lane?

_____

_____

_____

_____

_____

_____

_____

6. Before you read this book, what were some things that hindered you from maximizing your potential? Are those things still valid?

_____

_____

_____

_____

_____

_____

_____

7. What are the ways that you can stay accountable on your journey to achieving your full potential?

Lightning Source UK Ltd.
Milton Keynes UK
UKHW012152151221
395648UK00001B/299